BLUE JEAN
BABY

Library of Congress Cataloging in Publication Data
Parmer, Sally
Blue Jean Baby: One Girl's Trip Through the 1960s L.A. Music Scene

ISBN: 1-4392-2982-1
EAN13: 9781439229828

Visit www.booksurge.com to order additional copies.

BLUE JEAN BABY

One Girl's Trip Through the 1960s L.A. Music Scene

Sally Parmer

*This book is dedicated to
the slim-hipped long-haired guys
who made the music
and
the desperate doe-eyed Canyon girls
who worshipped them.*

Table of Contents

SECTION THREE
The Last Gasps of the Sixties

Preface

"A Generation Lost in Space"
Don McClean

L egendary disc jockey and show host Casey Kasem said the 1960s actually began around 1963 and ended about 1973. It was a time of change, and the change happened fast. Within two years a pervasive shift in consciousness was underway. And the first chords of a rock music evolution would define the beginning of a decade that would leave the world changed forever.

My generation carried the banner that transitioned western culture from conservative, post-war blandness to open-minded pro-activity. That transition included a free-spirited attitude toward speech, style, and behavior, and made the world cool for the first time since the 1920s.

In a recent Los Angeles seminar survey of people ages fourteen to eighty-one, derogatory words such as "dirty," "cheap," and "immoral" topped the list applied to the term "1960s female music fan." It seems as if, over the decades, the media has created a hardcore female groupie image of those of us involved in the 1960s music scene. In reality, the original music fans, those of us who hooked up with musicians in the early 1960s, were wide-eyed kids overwhelmed by a style of music so intensely life-affirming we longed to attach ourselves to the people who created the sound.

In the 1950s and early 60s, children gave their elders credit for life experience, honored those in positions of authority, kept the radio to a murmur, attended charm school, wore petticoats and white gloves to church, thanked God for the broccoli on their dinner plates, ranked chores before pleasure, attended ballroom dance lessons, practiced proper etiquette, and otherwise behaved like somewhat short adults.

Parents and teachers loudly and legally delivered punishment any way they saw fit, and children rarely dared to complain. Homes were run according to a schedule laid down by adults. Families washed and dressed before sharing breakfast and dinner. Women weren't pregnant, they were "blessed," as if by divine intervention. School campuses were chained and deadbolted during the day, and students were suspended for breaking dress and behavior codes. Sex was the 'S' word. Girls required school permission to wear earrings in pierced ears. Drugs were pills prescribed by the family doctor, and label instructions were followed to the letter. Those other, terrifying drugs like marijuana were mentioned only during the infamous sex education films of health class. Both drugs and sex were deadly; those films proved it.

The first groupies were innocent girls who wanted to meet musicians. An older, bolder, and sometimes amoral brand of music fan evolved during the late sixties and seventies, but those of us who spawned the flower child movement were actually baby boomers as the term was originally defined; it meant we were born between 1945 and 1951. We entered the world at the end of WWII, and maintained our parents' sense of propriety, even after trading perky flowered bell-bottoms for tight jeans with chain belts. We were innocent and played by the rules, woefully blind to the fact that the world was about to do a one-eighty.

SECTION ONE
Beatlemania and Other Childhood Diseases

Chapter One

"Good Morning Little Schoolgirl"
Ten Years After

During the last of the fifties and the early sixties, the world was a wasteland of dullness. The most outrageous trend since the beatnik era was a brief beach party fad that left most partygoers and film fans lying by the ocean in padded bathing suits and teased hair, yawning. It was time for things to happen, for the gods of inspiration to come up with something people could fall in love with again. Life was dull and we were bored. Even the war was cold.

In those early sixties, I began freshman year of high school wearing a homemade shirtwaist dress, T-strap flats, lavender eye shadow, and a modified Jackie Kennedy bouffant. My world had just been blown away by *West Side Story*, and I'd upgraded from classic ballet to wicked jazz dance class with its hip twitches and pelvic thrusts. I was so taken by the decadence of dancing street gangs that I aspired to become a badass. At five foot nine, 110 pounds, with auburn hair and Rinso white skin, it was going to be a stretch. I snuck pilfered cigarettes into the girls' restroom and began dropping terms like "hip" and "jazzy." Fellow *West Side Story* fanatic and dancer Lue joined me in this pursuit of badness, not an easy transition in the midst of sunny Southern California goodness.

We lived in a white middle-class neighborhood. There were two Asians and three Latinos at South High, and we'd never met an African American face-to-face. Family life was, in essence, still stuck in the 1950s. Every family dinner table featured meatloaf and macaroni at least once a week. A wild day involved a well-executed dance recital or a Saturday spent at the movies with a Coke and several boxes of Red Hots. Lue and other girlfriends surfed, the typical Southern California beach pastime for sports-minded natives with easily-tanned skin. I modeled for Teen Mannequins, a great little moneymaking venture for Southern California girls with an unbeachlike haute couture look.

How would we ever cop the title "bad?" Lue decided we should start with "it," which meant regular, serious necking that might someday lead to sex. She hooked up with a guy who wore a real leather jacket and combed his hair like Elvis. Hoods were rare. The only other two on campus included one who was unforgivably old at sixteen, and another who was five foot two to my five foot nine. "It," for me, was going to have to wait.

On an Indian-summer day in freshman Spanish class, our teacher was called to the office. Left to practice the latest dialogue, the class wouldn't have thought to take advantage of the teacher being gone. My dialogue partner and I had already nailed the lesson and been graded, leaving us time to talk. Although Jeanne seemed dismally uninteresting, on that particular day I noted something familiar in her. She had the look I saw in my own eyes when I gazed in the mirror. It screamed of unfulfilled need and desperate anticipation. Jeanne and I held a brief discussion about the state of our lives, and from that day on, whenever we took our seats in Spanish class, I'd swear, "Something has to happen; something big has to happen." Jeanne always nodded. She, like Lue and I, felt an unexplainable lack.

Either I was prophetic or manifested a miracle. Gossip about a group called the Beatles suddenly hit the West Coast of the United

States. Fashion magazines displayed British guys sporting collarless suits and girls with straight shoulder-length hair. British entertainment reporters declared they hadn't heard fans screaming since Elvis hit the scene a decade before, but the screaming had returned. The Beatles, the Rolling Stones, and nameless groups we'd soon grow to worship caused the ground to rumble in that West Coast pre-earthquake way. Something big was finally happening, and the emotionally weary among us vowed to be involved.

The first Beatles and Stones songs to hit L.A. radio were the antithesis of the surf, Motown, and do-wop we were used to. While the new sound was upbeat in content, we felt a visceral undertone. And we liked it.

I'd always wanted to work with music. This was not a dream, it was an intention. From an early age, I danced twice a week to classical music hammered out on an ancient piano, and I grudgingly carried my violin to school Mondays, Wednesdays, and Fridays. (I'd wanted to learn guitar.) My sister, Ann, sang in the church choir and L.A. theater performances. Paul, my brother, had a remarkable voice and proved to be the highlight of school assemblies. Our favorite aunt, Es, was once with a string quartet and still played violin. Pop (my grandfather) left the legacy of his booming voice on a set of red vinyl records. Daddy (never Dad or Father) was a blue-collar worker with a secret passion for opera, jazz, folk, and musical theater. When Mom first fell for his intense green eyes and Clark Gable grin, Daddy was renting a one-room cold water flat above an opera house. On their first date, Daddy shared his obsession with Mom by coercing her into risking her one silk dress and patent leather shoes on a rusty fire escape that led to an exit door of the theater. Music was a family obsession.

Although there was a phonograph in the living room, Daddy and I disappeared into the garage on Sunday afternoons, where a new hi-fi and two cherished reel-to-reel tape recorders were stashed. Daddy came alive in that garage. After bastardizing Cinderella in the world's worst fourth grade stab at musical theater, I decided to write musicals for a living. My early attempts were applaudable in length, but pitiable in content. Still, I could dance, sing, and play a musical instrument, and I lived in Los Angeles. I just needed to find a way to exploit this geographical advantage. Four lower-middle-class guys from a little place called Liverpool were changing the face of popular music. I was determined to learn from them.

About twice a week I stopped at the Woolworth's next to South High for a fresh pair of nylons. Pantyhose hadn't yet been invented, and either socks ("Oh, Mom, only spaz's wear socks!") or nylons were required school garb. While cracking gum in the checkout line one fateful afternoon, I spotted what appeared to be a box of trading cards. Lue shouted. They were Beatle pictures, and close-ups at that! I forewent the nylons, snags could always be repaired with clear nail polish, and handed over my two quarters for a Beatles photo. It was a purchase of ultimate importance.

Lue and I spent the late afternoon on her bedroom floor with the California sun lighting the faces of these four guys across the world in Liverpool, England. They were ugly. I searched for anything handsome, cute, or even interestingly likeable in any of the faces, and decided George was marginally acceptable. After serious deliberation, Lue settled on Paul because, as she sighed, "He might have some potential." I drifted home studying those four faces I knew I had to learn to love.

The 45rpm single of "I Want To Hold Your Hand" backed with "She Loves You" hit the local record store with a reverberating bang, and there went another fifty cents. *Meet The Beatles*, the long-awaited LP, had a rumored release date of one month. My heart raced at the anticipation of getting my hands on Beatle music. This new obsession was going to require money and freedom and I had neither. Mom ruled the household and everyone in it. I had to find a method of squeezing my way into her fading good graces, a trick that ranked just under impossible. Two years prior, my sister got married and my mother gave birth to my brother, who was a completely unexpected menopausal gift. When Paul was born my mother felt she had finally fulfilled her duty as a woman by giving birth to a son, but she was pushing fifty and no longer had the patience or perseverance to deal with this tiny creature. Her solution was alcohol, lots of it, which turned out, in odd ways, to be a temporary blessing. I no longer existed to either of my parents, or to my grandmother and favorite aunt Es who shared the house with us.

Prior to Paul's birth I'd been scrubbed clean, my curls had been chopped short with kitchen shears, and my clothes had been homemade. I now drew a heavy black line over green eyes, wore Erace cover-up like lipstick, and ironed my hair stick-straight on the ironing board, often laying the iron down on my hand. (It was painfully obvious who ironed their hair; we sported blisters on the tops of our left-hand fingers.) J.C. Penney accepted my two dollars in exchange for a black turtle neck top, which I paired it with an A-line skirt run off on my grandmother's sewing machine. I analyzed the completed image in the hallway mirror and compared it to a *Vogue* magazine photo of Jane Asher, Paul McCartney's girlfriend. This image was far cooler than Anita's and Maria's from *West Side Story,* and I thought I might be able to pull it off.

My sister's daughter had grown beyond infancy, and Ann became a bunny at the new L.A. Playboy Club. She and my brother-in-law often hired me to babysit, which was a godsend. Not only did I fill my pockets with dollar bills, I was able to temporarily escape the clutches of my mother. Mom had morphed into a mean drunk and the entire family was afraid of her. The household had always lived by her standards; now we were struggling to keep abreast of her ever-changing rules. My sister had been a few weeks pregnant at her wedding; this so embarrassed Mom that it was decided I would not date at all, ever. And because my sister had been in a minor fender bender while in high school, Mom declared I would not have a driver's license until I left home, a date she obviously longed for. Rules were laid down fast and hard, and with the blissful exceptions of one hour after school, daytime hours on weekends, and babysitting breaks, I was trapped.

Freshman science was a yawn of a class. The class sat trapped in a small, stuffy room on the far side of the campus and listened to the uninspired instructor drone on, day after day. One day in fall things changed. Within thirty minutes the room became unseasonably hot and still. It was earthquake weather. We all noticed the atmospheric shift, and as the teacher begged us to settle down, a kid from the office ran in, sweat soaking the front of his shirt. President Kennedy had been shot. A breathless ten minutes later we heard JFK was dead. Everything went silent. The teacher, hands shaking, excused herself to use an asthma inhaler. The kid from the office stood mutely at the front of the class. His left eye was twitching. The rest of us sat glued to our seats, stunned, until Theresa let out a shriek and began sobbing. The teacher begged her to see the nurse, but Theresa screamed she needed to go to church. The entire student body was herded onto the main lawn, where a group of Marines lowered the flag to half-mast.

I aimlessly made my way home alone that day, thinking how oddly appropriate it seemed that no children were playing ball in the streets, no dogs snoozing in the yards, no cars cruising through the neighborhood. Fires in the canyons created a haze that made the setting sun appear huge and bloody. The strangeness of that Twilight Zone day stuck with me, and earthquake weather still takes me back to the fateful incident that began one of the most remarkable decades in history.

Excitement replaced our sorrow when a closed circuit Beatles concert telecast was scheduled at the Redondo Beach Fox Theater. Tickets went on sale that Saturday morning at 10:00. Vickie, a new chum, tapped on my door at 5:00 a.m. I was made up and miniskirted ("mini" then meaning just above the knee). By 5:05, our Cuban heels were crunching rock-strewn asphalt. We were second in line. Dark and lanky Tina Van Voorhees was already standing at the theater doors. We looked each other over and decided to get along. During the first chilly hour of waiting, the three of us were alone against the brick wall. We swapped phone numbers, gossiped about the Beatles, and swore not to give anybody cuts in line.

By the time a crush of girls invaded the lobby at 10:10, Jeanne had spotted us and we climbed into the balcony. The Fox was an old, weather-worn theater on the beach, once magnificent. The front row of the balcony provided a great view, and Vickie's and Jeanne's screams echoed shrilly from on high.

I wasn't a screamer or a crier. Shouting to the images on the screen seemed futile. Instead I wanted to curl my fingers around the music and clutch it to my heart. But Vickie decided I wasn't displaying enough enthusiasm, so I stood to shout to a group of friends in the seats below. Leaning over the balcony railing was a bad idea. The stress of supporting a row of rabid teenage girls had exhausted the rotted wood, so when I added my 110 pounds there was a creak, followed by a crack. The railing swung away from the left side, about four feet out into space, with me attached. With a frantic kick I sent myself backward, and a burly usher grabbed my legs, pulling me onto the balcony. The ushers on either end of our section bellowed for everyone to stay seated, and for an annoying fifteen minutes a trio of workers hammered, glued and duct-taped. It was merely cosmetic. For the rest of the show we stayed put.

Jeanne and I began concert hopping, which was okay with Mom as long as the concert took place during the day, in a public venue, and Jeanne's mom dropped us off and picked us up. We sat through Dick and Dee Dee, James Brown, Jerry Lee Lewis, and anybody else who came to Los Angeles. I was thrilled by the experience of live rock music, no matter who was making it or how it sounded. Amazingly, I found rock-and-roll concerts to be even better than the ballet. I was hooked.

Chapter Two

"The Way You Walk, The Way You Talk "
Creedence Clearwater Revival

Hollywood was humming. British and faux-British groups popped up in every venue, including quickly-reconverted warehouses. Surfers let their hair go dark, bought guitars, and faked Cockney accents. Electronic squeals and off-key renditions of "She Loves You" and "Mona" echoed from suburban garages. Even the guys were gearing up for the arrival of the Beatles and the Stones. South High yearbooks were handed out in late spring, and mine was soon filled with hand-scribbled good wishes for the upcoming British rock star hunt. I'd finally fallen for The Beatles, but changed my loyalty from George to Ringo on the teenage rationalization he'd be easier to meet. I didn't care about autographs; I wanted to be part of the crowd that made the music.

Although there was great local music at the pier, the real L.A. music scene was Sunset Strip. On Saturdays we sat our fourteen-year-old butts on a northbound bus for thirty minutes, hopped off, rolled up the waistbands of our skirts, and applied heavier makeup. We were on the prowl for real rock stars, in the flesh.

It took about a month for us to admit the young girl/real rock star ratio was not in our favor. Girls who hung out with musicians had either talent or connections, so close friend Katy and I decided to take up guitar. We sang folk music already, a counterpoint to my jazz dancing and her cheerleading. Katy was blessed with a remarkable soprano vibrato and I had a decent contralto. Our harmony was unique. Katy spent three sweaty weekends working for her older brother and bought a cheap guitar with her earnings. She was learning the basics and I promised to catch up. After watching me relentlessly wash cars, scrub floors, babysit, and still come up short, my grandmother offered to help me buy an inexpensive guitar as an early holiday gift. Despite my mother's dread, I tuned the guitar, flawlessly picked out "Five Hundred Miles" on the first try, then worked out the song's four chords. Katy and I got our hands on *American Folk Classics*, some third-hand Bob Dylan sheet music, and a Peter, Paul and Mary songbook. We committed to memory every currently recognizable tune in the stack. It wasn't British music, it wasn't even rock music, but in six weeks we were playing for tips on stage at the Pizza Palace.

My first personal break came late one afternoon outside Jeanne's Beverly Hills dentist's office. A group of kids were sitting with a weary-looking nanny. Eventually one wire-toothed girl cautiously approached, giggled at me, and asked, "Are you Cher?" I was caught so off guard that I simply stared dumbly at her. Since when did I look like Cher, and why would anyone give a damn? We knew Sonny and Cher as Caesar and Cleo, a yawn-provoking opening act to be tolerated rather than applauded. Cher's hair was then barely mid-back, about the same length as my grown-out Jackie Kennedy bouffant from last summer, and Cher wore tacky dresses on stage. More recently, however, she had been showing up in magazines with heavy eye makeup and sleeker hair; she'd taken the British look and made it her own. That night I found a photo of Cher, checked out her bone structure and shape, and thought I might be able to take advantage of the resemblance.

My mother slapped down my request to darken my hair and, always suspicious, warned me she'd better not find any bottles of dye in the trash. I started buying "Raven" hair color capsules at a nickel a piece from Woolworth's. The gelatin capsules thankfully dissolved under hot water, so Mom couldn't prove anything. Within a month I went from medium-auburn to shiny black. When Mom demanded an explanation for this somewhat drastic change, I calmly explained it was hormones. Mom considered *hormones* a dirty word, but understood my theory. We'd been watching the sex ed films in health class, and I'd been armed with convincing information. I had Cher hair, and unless Mom wanted to root around in the shower drain for evidence, she was defenseless.

Most television shows and many magazines were still in black and white, so no one noticed I was green-eyed and fair-skinned and Cher was brown-eyed with darker skin. They noted our hair, cheekbones, shapes, and images, which were remarkably similar. The longer and darker my hair, the funkier my clothes, and the more makeup I applied, the more I heard, "You look just like Cher."

That image literally became my ticket to shows, excellent service at downtown shops, and free meals at Hamburger Hamlet on Sunset. Cher was becoming just popular enough that most people knew of her, and I was a good enough replica to be mistaken for her. Sometimes a doorman would declare, "Everybody pays here," or otherwise reject attempts at preferential treatment, but as long as I didn't smile (my smile was different from Cher's) my impersonation was typically convincing. I even sounded like Cher, an observation that inspired my science teacher's theory that Cher and I must have come from the same gene pool. She and I both had French ancestry, so maybe there was something to it. I didn't care. I just knew the resemblance opened doors.

Beatles concert tickets were scheduled to go on sale, and would undoubtedly sell out within the first few hours. Since it was illegal for underage kids to camp out overnight, hitting the asphalt at daybreak was the only option. Jeanne and I were already set. Loud, wealthy, and with a heart of Jell-o, Jeanne's father knew how to pull strings and had reserved a pair of box seats for us before the tickets were even printed.

The Beatles concert was slated for August, but we wanted to see them sooner. Jeanne's mother, always willing to accommodate her only child, agreed to book a Las Vegas trip with us. This coup would allow us to see the Beatles two full days before our friends in Los Angeles. I had to score airfare money, the biggest chunk of change I'd ever faced. Even more difficult, I needed permission, and Mom didn't trust me as far as she could spit. After a talk with my father, who said, "Aw hell, let her go," and a long discussion with Jeanne's parents, Mom agreed. In the interim I labored under the constant threat of that permission being revoked.

With one obstacle overcome, I moved on to the next: money. The lady next door taught office skills at a local high school. Her husband did his accounting work from home. He was a severely diabetic amputee with an understandably caustic nature. Mrs. Stoddard was obviously overworked. I often waved to her from my bedroom window late at night as she multi-tasked.

We cracked a deal. Mrs. Stoddard offered me minimum wage to grade student papers the rest of the semester and during summer school. My office skills were strong and Mrs. Stoddard knew she could trust me. Simple math proved that babysitting money, tips from singing, and Mrs. Stoddard's weekly chunks of cash would cover the trip to Las Vegas.

I received a startlingly late and frantic phone call from Jeanne the night prior to our trip. Had I packed enough makeup? Was I bringing my blue dress? Should we bother with bathing suits? Jeanne traveled at least twice a month, I'd never been anywhere, and she was asking me? We ended up taking everything in our closets, and in the two days and nights we were gone, we never even took off our shoes.

On the jarring small-plane ride to Vegas we met two girls from a local high school, Nina and Barbara. Nina and I clicked right off, and she showed me her latest secret purchase, a very British-mod pair of black lace stockings. Seeing us talking, a girl from the front of the plane asked to join the conversation. Cathy was a year younger than the rest of us, naturally blond and dewy-eyed.

She was a very young freshman at a nearby Catholic school, and couldn't wait to see the Beatles. Jeanne and I thought we were doing something exclusive by going to Las Vegas, but here we were in a group. We just hoped the group stayed small.

Although Jeanne's dad grumbled that he could have scored free rooms at the Stardust, he'd been convinced to book us at the Sahara where the Beatles were staying. We cursed the fact that we had a bungalow, however, because the Beatles would be staying in the main tower. We had a clear view of their rooms from our deck, but Jeanne convinced me it would be an impossible climb. Even if I managed to crawl from balcony to balcony, Sahara security would certainly shoot me down like King Kong.

Nina, Barbara, Jeanne, and I crowded together in a hotel restaurant booth for lunch. Nina spotted Pat Boone at a table by the windows, and we asked our waitress if Mr. Boone would be willing to talk with us. Our favorite L.A. radio station had held a huge contest for passes to Pat Boone's Las Vegas Beatle party, scheduled for tonight. When the waitress waved us over, we descended en masse, determined to talk our way into invitations.

Pat Boone laughed and denied knowledge of a party. Initially we thought he was avoiding a potential party-crashing, but within a couple of minutes Mr. Boone's manager showed up with the declaration that it was time to catch the plane back to Los Angeles. There was no party.

We respected and trusted the disc jockeys of the early 1960s. Radio personalities weren't teenage music fans fresh out of trade school or unemployed actors marking time; they were older, educated, and took their jobs seriously. Many of them had substantial journalism backgrounds, and deserved to be honored for their work. Now, after learning that all the hype surrounding the Beatle party contest was bogus, we didn't know what to think. I walked out, my sandwich untouched and unpaid for, and my friends forgotten. It was an unmannerly thing to do, but I'd been completely disillusioned. In five fleeting minutes, I'd begun to view the world in a much more cynical way.

Walking back toward the bungalow, I caught Cathy's diminutive shadow. She was leaning against a white wall, and summoned me with her index finger. We'd all figured the Beatles would arrive at the main hotel entrance red carpet style, but Cathy somehow knew they were being smuggled in at night. After scribbling a note for Jeanne and her parents, Cathy and I walked the perimeter of the Sahara creating a crude blueprint of the buildings and their entrances and exits. If they actually wanted security, the Beatles were going to have to enter at one of two loading docks. We established Plan A and Plan B. This was serious business.

Jeanne, Nina, and Barbara were sworn to secrecy because there were, according to the news, about five hundred girls swarming around the Sahara. Jeanne's parents made us promise we'd shower and eat a reasonable dinner. They just did not comprehend that we couldn't chance being otherwise occupied when the Beatles arrived. Because we did have a clear view of the main tower from our deck, Jeanne and I paced there with our radio tuned to the news, watching a rising thermometer partially hidden by a wasp-infested shrub.

It was just after 11:00 p.m. and 105 degrees when the local radio broadcaster announced that the Beatles had arrived at the airport. We watched wispy shadows of girls cruising the sidewalks, but no cheer went up; there was no response to the news. Why was everything so still? We had no idea if the Beatles would be detained in celebrity holding while luggage was dealt with, or if they'd come straight to the hotel. Obviously Cathy had some secret source of information, but no one answered the phone in her room. Shortly before midnight, Nina tip-toed up, whispered, "Plan A," and vanished into the night. I hopped the low fence onto the sidewalk. Jeanne tried to follow and split her skirt all the way up the side. I was poised, ready to run screaming to the main tower service elevator dock, but waited the couple of minutes it took for Jeanne to change. We sprinted, which to our dismay attracted followers. An original group of twelve girls grew to thirty by the time a black limo pulled in just after midnight.

I was pinned against the passenger side, staring into John Lennon's remarkable eyes. The overhead lights created a weird blue cast, and the Beatles looked unnatural, like department store mannequins. I felt as if I were being rude, crushed up against the window like that, so I smiled dumbly at John, who smiled back. He mouthed what I assumed was "Hello," and I shouted, "Nice to meet you!" It was one of those car wreck time-warp moments. I was face-to-face with a Beatle, and all I'd managed was a courteous "Nice to meet you." I felt like an idiot.

Obviously the hotel hadn't anticipated anyone figuring out their not-so-grand scheme. One plump middle-aged cop was the only security available to fend off thirty adrenalin-hyped teenage girls. George, sandwiched between two men in suits, was hustled around behind me. I was yanked out of the way so John could exit the car. I wrestled free and did a nice pas de chat that allowed me to clamp my right hand onto John's left shoulder, just as the cop shot out both arms, catching me square in the face. I followed through with a petit battement to the back of his knee. I'd had my clutches on a Beatle, and this jerk had interfered. It was too late to try again. The Beatles were in the elevator.

Nina, Cathy, and I clasped hands at the back of the service entrance, bemoaning the fact that this pursuit of real rock stars was going to require more skill and treachery than anticipated. Jeanne showed up a minute later, crying hysterically. She'd managed to grab Paul McCartney and plant a kiss on him. It was kind of funny, even childish, but damn! She'd kissed a Beatle! Nina pointed out that Barbara was missing. Big, dumb, oafish Barbara seemed to have disappeared. Oh God, what had she done? Did any of us know how to post bail? A tense five minutes later, our missing friend staggered out of the elevator, clutching her comb. There were black eyeliner-tears on her cheeks. "I combed their hair!" she gasped. "They just stood and smiled all the way up and let me comb their hair!" Barbara had a comb full of Beatle hair. We'd bagged our first moose.

Jeanne's parents created a formidable barrier to our room, but all was forgiven when they learned we'd seen the Beatles. Jeanne's mom had us verify we'd eaten dinner (we hadn't), and promise that we'd shower before going to sleep (we wouldn't). We managed to brush our teeth and hair, but lay on our beds fully clothed. If there was a Beatle sighting, we'd be there pronto. We lay in the dark, sticky from heat and excitement, conversation low and intermittent. Sleep escaped us both.

Early in the morning Jeanne's mother had breakfast sent to our room. How could we "chase the Beatles" if we didn't eat? Jeanne and I picked at unwanted cinnamon rolls until the ring of our phone broke the boredom. It was Mom. She completely floored us by saying we'd made L.A. TV news, and that photos of the crowd around the Beatles limo hit the local newspapers. I thought it was a bad joke. How could we have been so focused on the Beatles that we overlooked major news media? Jeanne and I didn't have time to analyze it. We touched up our makeup and left.

Chapter Three

"Here, There, and Everywhere"
The Beatles

It was immediately obvious that the main tower was under top security. Several guards and a couple of scowling cops were posted at the doors, and entrance to the elevator required a main tower room key. Cathy whispered that to get onto the Beatles floor your key had to bear the appropriate floor stamp, making me wonder yet again where she got her amazingly accurate information. There were different colored keys for the various parts of the hotel. Our silver-tone keys indicated we had bungalows, copper keys were given to those with second-tower rooms, and the now-coveted shiny gold keys gave holders access to the main tower. Ours suddenly seemed pale and impotent.

Jeanne suggested going to a locksmith and having a copy made in the appropriate color, so we caught a cab and found a dirty little key shop. The unshaven guy behind the counter said he couldn't copy room keys, and even if he could, why did we want one in a different color? Jeanne and I stepped aside and weighed our options. Maybe we could pay Vito here to copy a housekey in gold, go elsewhere, and have it stamped with an appropriate room number. Jeanne clutched my arm at the sight of a familiar girl. We watched

Pattie Boyd, George Harrison's girlfriend, as she laid down her room key and asked to have it reproduced in gold. What was going on?

After being rejected, she and her companion turned toward the door and saw us. The girls hesitated briefly before asking me if I could get them into the main tower. "Aren't you staying with George?" I asked. Pattie started laughing. "Oh God, you're not Cher, are you? I just assumed." The four of us had gotten completely confused. Pattie Boyd wasn't Pattie Boyd. According to her story, she was Pattie's cousin. Jeanne and I shot each other suspicious looks. Was the accent real? During the past few months, fake British accents had bloomed like dandelions. Was this perky little blonde just another impersonator like me? We told the girls we couldn't get into the main tower, either. The four of us shared a cab back to the Sahara, where Jeanne and I lagged behind, curious as to what the other girls might try. They were obviously older than us and probably had more experience with real rock stars.

Several rows of girls stood in audience as Ringo ate breakfast on his balcony. Every few minutes, he'd wave to the crowd below, and a cheer would go up. One of the Beatles was just now eating, and the concert wasn't until early afternoon. It was a reasonable assumption the other Beatles were in their rooms, too. The girl who claimed to be Pattie's cousin, in a somewhat-stilted accent, began shouting, "George, it's Pattie's cousin!" Jeanne and I decided she was wasting her voice, but ate our words later when the two older girls were seen exiting the main tower, disheveled and smelling of men's cologne, giggling with delight.

Nina's mother had taken her shopping, and Barbara and Jeanne claimed to be starving. They were both certain that access to the main tower was impossible. Promising my friends I'd catch up with them inside the restaurant, I went in search of Cathy.

Shrieking and giggling girls had gathered in the lobby of the main tower, and my breath caught in my throat. But the attraction was just a couple of long-haired guys in sunglasses, posing for photos with some of the giddier kids. I found Cathy escaping the scene. When she saw me, we grabbed each others hands, and simultaneously demanded, "You're not giving up, are you?" Vowing we'd find a way into that main tower, we parted company to prepare for the concert.

I'd experienced the screaming crowds at the closed-circuit concert and joined in the thrill of the *Ed Sullivan Show* performance. By contrast, the Las Vegas Convention Center seemed disappointingly quiet. Many audience members were older people who'd come out of curiosity. The clean-cut guy next to me was a Las Vegas native who bought a ticket at the last minute, just to salvage an unscheduled afternoon. Two lone cops leaned against the stage, looking dead bored. There were excited screams, but only at the beginnings of songs, as girls recognized their favorites.

Jeanne, having practiced screaming at home with the doors and windows shut, bellowed, "Paul!" and miraculously, Paul looked up, smiled, and nodded. I waited. I also wanted Beatle attention, but with my thin folk-singer voice I had to struggle to be loud. At the end of Ringo's heartwarming "This Boy," something apparently came unplugged, because there was a rude electronic squeal followed by a long pause. George was standing center stage in the quiet auditorium. I jumped up, shook my hands in the air, and shouted, "George! Play 'All My Lovin'!" He frowned. I didn't know if he was angry or if he hadn't heard me, so I yelled again. And, by God, the guys went into "All My Lovin." It may have been next on their schedule, but I felt I'd gotten a special request through to the Beatles, and I was thrilled.

Post-concert, the Sahara was overrun with young girls. Three feathered and glittered showgirls were ushered into the main tower elevator, and everyone knew where they were headed, damn it. Seeing those glamorous older women being taken to the Beatle rooms was disheartening, although deep inside I was still convinced that there was a way for us peasants to access those suites, too.

Jeanne's parents insisted we have dinner with them because, after all, we'd seen the concert. Nina and Barbara were in the restaurant with Nina's parents, and Cathy sat two tables away across from her mother. Other girls sullenly picked at food ordered by their own parents. The room looked like a Mayberry potluck festival. Because the concert was over we were expected to calm down and return to normal life. We were amazed at our parents' naiveté. Life would never be normal again. We hadn't traveled to Las Vegas to attend a concert. We'd each come to meet, sleep with, and marry a Beatle.

Jeanne and I paced our deck, watching shadows cross the windows in the Beatle rooms. Every now and then, Ringo leaned out to toss a handful of rings onto the grass below. Jeanne encouraged me to nab a Ringo ring as a souvenir, but my mind was elsewhere. Sure, as Jeanne moaned, the Beatles were a million floors straight up in a secured building. That was one way of looking at it. But I chose to focus on the fact that they were right there.

That evening, Jeanne's father took off for a comedy revue, but her mom stayed in. She wanted to rest and thought we should do the same. Jeanne curled up in front of the TV, but I noticed she didn't remove her shoes. I spent an irritating forty-five minutes trying to phone Nina and Cathy. Finally, around nine, Cathy responded. The Beatles were leaving in the morning. Cathy and I were booked on the 1:00 flight back to LAX. I was trapped for the night, but we synchronized watches and promised to meet at 6:30 a.m. We would beg, cry, or bully our way into that main tower.

At 6:00 a.m., Jeanne's father stomped into our room and demanded we each shower. How could we stand ourselves? We were always so fussy about morning ablution. What were we thinking? (Oh, if he only knew.) When Jeanne and I were alone, we turned on the shower, practiced feminine hygiene, rolled down our nylons long enough to shave our legs, brushed our teeth and hair, and applied more makeup; by now we'd caked on so much mascara we struggled to keep our eyes open. Deodorant, cologne (Revlon's "Oh, de London!"), and we hit the sidewalk running.

Cathy, Jeanne, and I were thrown off-balance by the sight of a security guard planted at the now-closed door to the main tower.

Cathy and I shot each other looks of panic when he asked to see our room keys. Not finding another option, we offered them up, gestured in the direction of our rooms, and oddly enough, that seemed to satisfy the guard. It was quiet inside. Only one woman stood behind the main desk, but there were two guards, arms crossed, at the elevator doors. Cathy and I agreed there was only one thing to do. We had to steal a key.

By mid-morning the floor was busy. Guests were requesting and returning keys and luggage was hustled in and out. As soon as time and luck allowed, one of us would have to create a diversion while the other nabbed a key.

Jeanne disapproved. Yes, she was in love with Paul McCartney and would die for the guy, but she wouldn't risk angering a desk clerk to get to him. I thought Jeanne should check her priorities, because the three of us needed to be in agreement. Nina and Barbara came to our rescue. They'd flown in to Las Vegas but were driving back to L.A. now. Nina promised to phone me at home the next day. When Jeanne offered to walk our two new friends to their rental car, Cathy and I exhaled with relief.

We scoped out the floor and decided we needed a major distraction. Within a minute, our prayers were answered. Shouts went up. The Righteous Brothers stopped briefly to sign autographs. Cathy and I started to move, but the crowd prevented us from getting to the keys behind the desk. I wanted to yell, "Get out of our way! Don't you know the Beatles are going to leave soon?" But we waited impatiently until the guys and their bodyguard exited the building and the crowd dispersed.

The hotel maids seemed to have unlimited access to the elevators, so for a brief moment we considered trying to find a maid's uniform. But the women were older, wore marginal makeup, and kept their hair piled up under hairnets; we would never pass.

We needed a key. A well-dressed young guy smiled, "Hey, Cher." I nodded. Cathy's eyes grew bright with inspiration. After a whispered instruction, I snatched up a house phone and insisted on being connected to Sonny Bono's room. Head down, straight dark hair swinging, I began shouting at some poor hotel operator who patiently tried to make sense of my ranting. Two minutes later, I apologized and hung up, only to turn and see Cathy showing her newly claimed key to an elevator guard. Two women approached and asked for my autograph, but I was already running, angry and desperate. Just before the elevator doors shut tight, a maid hugged me against her and loudly declared, "You're going to lose your roommate." This aproned angel shoveled me, her laundry cart, and herself into the elevator. The guards didn't say a word. Cathy knew I was mad, and justifiably so. She opened her hand to display a fourth-floor key. Damn, that wasn't going to work. The maid noticed too, however, and took the key from Cathy's hand, replacing it with her own Beatle floor key.

We reverently stepped out onto the Beatles' floor. I turned to thank the maid, who quickly put a finger to her lips. She nudged me along the hallway to a suite of rooms. Two other maids looked up fearfully. We'd caught them stashing ashtrays, napkins, and washcloths into their pockets. My personal angel left for a minute, then returned with the grave news that the Beatles had left the tower minutes earlier by a different exit. She then pointed out which room had belonged to what Beatle. Ringo's rooms were already picked clean. Cathy kept her eyes averted as she collected pieces of a broken drinking glass she then tried to stash in the pillow case I'd pulled off John Lennon's bed. "No," I hissed, grabbing the pillowcase and emptying it, "this one's mine." I had John Lennon's pillowcase and knew I had to hike it if I was going to see the Beatles drive away.

I was angry, tired, and rushed, and began nudging people out of the way, something I would never have thought to do forty-eight hours earlier. I know I shoved comedian Buddy Hackett because Jeanne's father got a photo of it and read me the riot act on rudeness.

Cars were lined up on either side of the long driveway. Still basically polite, we girls honored the makeshift metal barricade that would separate us from our heroes. I squeezed in behind a shiny white luxury sedan just as George, Paul, and John walked by, smiling and waving to the crowd. My heart sank. I'd missed Ringo, my favorite Beatle. The man I was sure would marry me if he only got to know me. I slumped back against a wall as a series of screams went up. And there he was, Ringo in the flesh. With a burst of adrenalin I hooked my toe on the ledge of the car window, leapt, and landed spread-eagle face-down on the roof of the blister-hot sedan. Ringo was within two feet of me. I screamed, "Ringo!" and shot out my hand to touch him, when my foot slipped and I began a hot and painful slide backward. Ringo paused, smiled, and reached out his hand, but it was too late. I was back on asphalt. As he walked away, he laughed, "You're good on your feet, luv."

Ringo had called me "luv." Suddenly all the scheming and conniving, the logical, left-brained Sally, was gone, and I understood how Jeanne felt after kissing Paul McCartney. It was a rush I'd never felt before. The boredom of the past few years was gone forever.

Thirty hard-earned dollars remained housed in my Lady Buxton. Jeanne's mother suggested I buy a newspaper headlining the mob of girls at the Sahara. Jeanne tried to con me into a pair of fly-eye sunglasses, so in style in London. I ended up buying an overpriced stuffed animal for my baby brother and pocketing the rest of the money. I'd gotten what I came for. I'd been through real rock star boot camp.

The flight back to Los Angeles was, in essence, a summit meeting. I traded Jeanne part of my prized John Lennon pillowcase for a ruffle we managed to tear from the blouse she was wearing, a part that had touched Paul McCartney. Cathy, who had been encouraged by Jeanne's mother to sit with us, called a truce with me. She'd betray her own mother in a hot second, but I agreed to her peace treaty; she was smart and somehow got access to information. Musician chasing wasn't going to be easy, and I needed my wagons in a circle.

An hour later, I stumbled into the living room, filthy and exhausted. My mother started to snap at me, but Daddy laughed and said I must have had a hell of a time. I'd gone two hot days and nights without sleep, and consumed the total of half a cinnamon bun, part of a bowl of soup, and three or four Cokes. I was wearing the same clothes I'd left in, and had mascara dandruff on my cheeks. All I wanted right then was to consume an entire bag of barbequed potato chips. Tomorrow was the Hollywood Bowl concert. I needed a long shower and a clean bed.

Chapter Four

"Stuck in the Middle with You"
The Steve Miller Band

Jeanne and I arrived at the Beatles concert two hours early. The Hollywood Bowl was famous for its symphonies and Easter sunrise services, but neither of us had been there before, so the geographic layout was unfamiliar. Other girls apparently suffered the same frustration. We asked one another about entrances, exits, and stage access, but no one seemed to have an answer. I began to lose enthusiasm. Of course it would be great to see the Beatles, but I'd already concluded we'd be staying in our seats tonight. Most ticket holders hadn't yet seen the Beatles, so excitement was high. Opening acts walked right through the crowd, almost unnoticed. Nobody cared about anything but the Beatles. They were the reason every seat had sold that first day.

An unfamiliar energy rose as night fell, a feeling I've rarely experienced. The air crackled like an electrical storm in the desert. For a smoggy L.A. night, it was remarkably easy to breathe. Colors were brighter than normal, sounds were more pleasant, and I kept smelling jasmine, although there was none around. A popular TV star sat with his wife in the box behind us, and seemed as thrilled to be there as the rest of us. Love floated in the air. Love and something I would later recognize as sexual energy. We were all pumping adrenalin, dancing on point, preparing to spring, so ready to devour the Beatles I almost felt sorry for the opening acts. No one was listening or offering much applause. We were waiting.

After a ridiculously long introduction that is better described as an ad for a sponsoring radio station, we heard the words, "And here they are, the Beatles!" If I'd been a screamer, I'd have shouted with everyone else. I think the opening song was "Twist and Shout," but screaming was all any of us really heard. It was a hot August night in Los Angeles, and the Beatles were singing their hearts out just for us. A girl from a front box jumped in the pond and tried to swim to the stage. Another girl fainted and was carried out unconscious. Las Vegas had become a dim memory. I was one of them now. I was a Beatlemaniac, unknowingly on my way to becoming a groupie.

By the end of summer I'd re-prioritized my life. For the first time since I was very small, I was no longer enrolled in dance class. Folk singing was a priority; not only did it bring in money, there was an off-chance someone might believe Katy and I had serious talent. I agreed to continue to work for Mrs. Stoddard, for the quick money, and I'd babysit my niece. I also took my sister's advice and got more seriously into modeling, saying my goodbyes to Teen Mannequins, and signing on with Grace Moorehead. It was further income and most of the Moorehead gigs took me to high profile salons and top end department stores downtown.

I gave up homework. As long as I remained alert in class and did well on exams I could get Bs and a few Cs; I didn't care about being college prep anymore. I had already decided to leave home the minute I turned eighteen, and was no longer sure college was in my future. My parents certainly wouldn't help pay for my education; everything went into trusts and other funds for my baby brother. He was the center of their lives now, and my future, academic and otherwise, meant nothing to them. As long as I followed their rules, maintained a low profile, and stayed out of trouble, I didn't exist.

My social life presented a different challenge. It was time to let Jeanne sink or swim; I loved her but wasn't willing to let her hold me back. The high school student body was comprised of cliques, and Jeanne, Carol, Debbie, and Margaret belonged to a different species; they were style-free and had different goals, ambitions, beliefs, and morals than Katy, Cheryl, Connie, and I. I also needed to avoid a new girl named Cathi who followed me around in a rude attempt to get and keep my attention; Katy called her my stalker. On the periphery of our clique were Linda, Vickie, Pam, Sandy, and a couple of others I didn't know well. Although they went to different schools, I stayed in touch with Nina, Cathy Costa, and Tina Van Voorhees. Then there were the two intriguing girls who worked alone. Girls I wanted to know. Rita was just starting high school, but she had a rocking woman's body and a wealthy uncle who worked with popular Los Angeles disc jockey Reb Foster. Yvette was already an active groupie and knew things I intended to learn.

I tapped my way through two typewriter ribbons, keeping notes and defining the rules as I understood them then. It all boiled down to a few basic concepts. It was best to surround yourself with girls equally smart but less cunning than you, because you didn't want somebody pulling a Cathy Costa stolen key getaway. It was good sense to make sure friends were equal in appearance to you; an ugly girl drew the interest level down to the lowest common denominator, and someone absolutely breathtaking made the rest of you pale in comparison. And it was a bad idea to hang around with giddy girls and screamers; you wanted to meet musicians, not have them sign your autograph book.

We stomped onto campus sophomore year in go-go boots, the shortest skirts we could get away with, and turtle neck tops. Earrings were hoops, preferably gold. And eye makeup was heavy. Shoulder bags replaced last year's clutches. The group of us was immediately identifiable as "them," as in, "Oh, you're one of them."

We pitied people who didn't understand us. Didn't they get goose-bumps listening to the guitar riff in "Words of Love?" Couldn't they feel the raw sexual energy in Mick Jagger's voice? They just didn't get it.

There was cement seating area in the middle of campus, where the rah-rahs and football jocks hung out. The rest of us typically steered clear of the area, but two new guys, both attractive and obviously not jocks, spent their lunch periods on the cement bench that first week. Steve and Willy just met; they were transfers from different high schools and didn't know they were sitting in the jock circle. Steve and Willy were seniors, and both managed to get away with hair several inches longer than school rules dictated. Steve was unarguably a gorgeous blond male specimen but Willy looked like a Beatle with his enviably shiny brown hair, vivid blue eyes, and killer smile. And he wore turtle necks and tweed jackets with jeans. Best of all, he had a great voice. He was currently in a local musical theater production, and sang out loud, often and shamelessly. Jeanne fell immediately in love with him.

My class schedule sent me all the way across the sprawling single-story campus between fourth and fifth periods. It required a near-sprint. When my bootheels hit the threshold, a cute blond guy in the back began singing "I Got You, Babe." As fate would have it, my seat was directly in front of his. John and his friends called me Cher, and I was getting tired of hearing, "Do you know who you look like?" One day, after John and three other guys nicely harmonized a soft medley of Sonny and Cher songs to the rhythm of the teacher's achingly dull lecture, I asked John to continue the singing but to please stop calling me Cher. He agreed, but started calling my Sonny instead. It was funny in math class, but the name spread all over campus.

I was laughing about this new name with Katy during lunch one day, when someone behind us began singing "Pick-a-Little-Talk-a-Little" from *The Music Man*. It was Willy. His family had moved in around the corner from Katy's house, and she'd recently gotten to know him. The three of us mulled over the validity of a nickname.

I hated my own name and always wanted a nickname, but was a nickname stupid or could it be cool? We knew a guy nicknamed Itchy, who played guitar and sang like Dylan. He was cool. And there was Corki, a perky little blond sweetheart of a girl whose real name was Harriet. Katy thought Sunny, with a "u," kind of suited me. In an attempt to help out, Willy asked my middle name, which I explained was Rebecca. That completely cracked him up. "Like *Rebecca of Sunnybrook Farm*?" he howled. From then on I was Sunnybrook. Jeanne, whose father flew to San Francisco twice a week, brought me empty airline-sized Sunnybrook liquor bottles. Gary, famous for the world's smallest graffiti (before anyone even knew what graffiti was) started printing "Sunnybrook" on lunch benches and restroom doors. "Sunny" stuck, but fortunately "Sunnybrook" stayed on campus, although Linda refers to me by that name to this day.

Life was still innocent and we were still kids. No matter what we tried to pull during the day, we made sure we were home before dark, although most of us were granted permission to spend Friday evenings at Reb Foster's new teenage nightclub, the Revelaire. The name was quickly shortened to the Rev. Rows of black lights hugged the walls, kids could dance however they wanted, and adults weren't allowed inside. Rita ran the concession stand. She was underage and lacking a work permit, making the situation illegal. Nobody even considered registering a complaint. No one was being abused.

Jeanne found out I knew Willy, and all of a sudden, I had a conjoined twin. I told her to come to the Rev on Friday and hang out with us, but Jeanne insisted she didn't dance. When I promised she could safely sit along the side wall with those just hanging out, she mutely shook her head. I finally introduced Jeanne to Willy after school one day, but Willy had a strange habit of simply disregarding people who didn't interest him, and Jeanne fell into that category. She seemed to think I could somehow force my new buddy to pay attention to her, although I barely knew him myself.

I couldn't afford Jeanne to be in one of her moods. Just a few weeks prior, life was on track, but between Jeanne and Mom, I'd been derailed again. My mother had the phone cord shortened from three feet to one foot, so anybody on our one telephone could be heard by everyone else in the house. Planning weekends, sleepovers, and other events was harder, but I kept my clipboard handy and used shorthand. I regularly found Mom going through my purse and pockets, so I chose to communicate privately at home via shorthand ("It's homework, Mom") and very poor high school Spanish ("Deje en paz mí, Madre").

Ian Whitcomb, part of what was now called the British invasion, was due to arrive in Los Angeles on Saturday. Jeanne thought Ian was "really really cute," so Katy and I took her to the airport in an attempt to jolly her up. LAX was a great place to meet and talk to guys like Peter and Gordon (Peter was always laid back and gracious, but Gordon was on a huge ego trip), and Chad and Jeremy (both were funny, and had gentle spirits). Some very popular Englishmen came through LAX with minor security. We fans were still baby boomers and, for the most part, respected authority and practiced manners.

We learned of Ian's arrival through a network we had developed with other real rock star fans. Although members of this network weren't necessarily close friends, we stayed in touch and traded favors and information. Tina Van Voorhees, the girl who'd been first in line at the closed circuit Beatle concert, had an aunt who worked in security at the airport, and Tina leaked out arrivals and departures in exchange for other real rock star information. We expected a small crowd the day Ian was due, so we were surprised to see about a hundred girls waiting. Something had gone wrong. A disc jockey at a college radio station had gotten wind of Ian's arrival and announced it on the air.

Although Ian actually was really really cute, Katy and I weren't big fans. His only hit was a novelty song; he didn't move us. Worse, we'd mistakenly heard he was gay. Ian approached the crowd, grinning and gracious, trying to shake as many hands and sign as many autographs as possible while being hustled along by his manager and another man. At the curb where Ian's car was waiting, the manager turned and held up a record album, announcing it was for Ian's fan club president, Kate. Apparently Kate had been detained, so Katy stepped up with Jeanne and me behind her. Ian's manager gave Katy an autographed album and handed the three of us tickets to the filming of a popular teenage music show, *Shivaree*.

We'd been to the filming of *Shindig* and seen an incredibly stoned and very pregnant Marianne Faithfull literally lifted into a chair for her song. We'd watched the Kinks climb into the rafters and chant, "My kingdom for a hump!" We'd witnessed the Animals fight with the production staff. But *Shivaree* was different, because some audience members were chosen to stand on stage with the performers, offering both exposure and real rock star contact.

On the day of filming, we got to the heavily-guarded TV studio in the early afternoon and immediately sent a message to Ian's manager. He asked us to wait for the show. Apparently fan club presidents, real or phony, didn't rank in the music world.

Katy and Jeanne found a doughnut stand and the three of us planted ourselves outside the studio gates for an impromptu picnic. A dozen doughnuts and two hours later, Ian and his manager came toward us. Ian called, "Which one of you is having a birthday?" and Katy immediately shouted, "I am!" All of us ran past the guards into a safe space between the two men. Some girl had shown up on her birthday, hoping to be treated to an autograph, and lost her opportunity to us. I felt a stab of remorse for her, but it didn't last. Being one of us required perseverance, and if you didn't have it, you were just out of luck.

Ian spent the afternoon playing ragtime piano. This bored Katy and Jeanne, but I had my dad's smaller reel-to-reel in my shoulder bag, and taped wonderful piano music, bawdy British drinking songs, and a lot of Ian's laughter.

Jeanne, Katy, and I were chosen to stand on stage during filming. I wanted my face on camera, so I planted myself next to one of the six-inch risers the performers stood on while singing. Unfortunately, I was standing next to Bobby Rydell's riser; he was just out of the service and had cut a new record. But he couldn't have been more than about five foot six, because in two-inch heels I looked like an amazon hovering over a dwarf, and so was excused to stand under one of the go-go dancers, the worst spot on stage. Both dancers had been drinking all day and it was obvious neither was wearing underwear. The day ended on a somewhat down note, although I did have my very cool tape of ragtime piano music.

On Friday night, a group of us went to the Rev. I don't know what had gotten into Willy, but he started teasing me and then kissing me. We wound up laughing and making out unknowingly in full view of Willy's steady girlfriend, who'd shown up as a surprise. I knew every high school in the area would hear about this minor tryst, and that Jeanne would be madder than hell.

They did and she was. Although Jeanne had only met Willy once, on campus, in broad daylight, with school rules forbidding anything more scandalous than hand holding, she wanted to know why Willy had never kissed her. She presented an updated image, and couldn't understand why guys just didn't like her. Jeanne was an only child and had been given everything a kid could want. She still expected to get what she wanted, so when things didn't fall in her lap, she played the huffy little princess.

So because Jeanne had a crush on Willy and he didn't return the compliment, she was angry that he had kissed me. This was a bad case of teenage logic. It was unbelievably petty, but it was happening. Cheryl said Jeanne needed to get laid. Although none of us had actually experienced sex yet, I knew what Cheryl meant; Jeanne needed defrosting. We didn't need this kindergarten social crisis. We all had tickets to the Stones concert and couldn't afford to have Jeanne spoil the day.

Chapter Five

"City Girls Just Seem to Find Out Early"
The Eagles

On a Saturday afternoon toward the end of the month, a group of us went to the Rev. The Turtles, who had recently changed their name from the Crossfires, were still the house band, and we typically sat in on weekend rehearsals. Mark and I necked a lot in those days. He phoned a couple of times a week, and he took me home with him several times for frantic making out, but I wouldn't have sex with him. Sure, he was a real rock star with some big hits, but he didn't seem like one. He was just a guy from my neighborhood who happened to be friendly, funny, and very talented. And he was fat, with bad hair. It just felt wrong. When I was with Mark, Howard was often groping Katy, and Rita was always with Ed. She and Ed had been an item for a long time.

At school on Monday, Katy, Connie, Cheryl, and I had a conference about Cathi. She didn't have the right image, with an unpleasantly upturned nose, ruddy skin that never quite looked clean, and clown-red hair that was fashionably long but terribly frizzy. And every day, rain or shine, Cathi wore a long, black, crinkled-vinyl coat that was supposed to look like leather. Worst of all, she insulted people, to their faces, all of the time. We just couldn't have her hanging around with us unless she made some drastic changes to both her appearance and her behavior. Since Cathi was my personal stalker, I was chosen to either get rid of her or fix her. Knowing Cathi would never leave us alone, I promised to have her dump the ugly coat, and knock off the unwarranted criticism. I also agreed to teach her to wear appropriate makeup and deal with her hair. When confronted, Cathi balked at the idea she wasn't perfect, and she went on the attack. After sitting through a ten-minute earful of criticism, I explained that the other girls just weren't willing to hang out with Cathi unless she made a few changes. She was visibly surprised, and finally agreed to accept my help.

Cathi disappeared from school for a couple of days and nobody bothered to phone her, assuming she was angry. No one wanted to listen to her criticism; we were all fed up with constant nasty remarks. When Cathi didn't show up the third day, her mother, Mrs. Willard, phoned me with the news that Cathi was too sick to leave alone. She asked me to bring the necessary schoolwork to the house. Mrs. Willard was sniffling, and the longer we talked, the more I was convinced she'd been crying. I showed up after school the next day with Cathi's lessons, and Mrs. Willard somberly sat me down next to her. Apparently Cathi had been so upset at our decision she'd tried to commit suicide. Mrs. Willard had found her unconscious on the bathroom floor in the middle of the night. The ER technicians pumped Cathi's stomach and found a fascinating combination of over-the-counter drugs. I swore to myself I'd never deliver hurtful news to anyone again, and I promised Mrs. Willard to keep quiet; I'd simply say Cathi had the flu. I left a note for Cathi to read when she woke up, swearing we would remain friends. And, like all mannerly girls born in the forties and raised in the fifties, I kept my word. This bit of compassion was a smart move because Cathi not only accepted my help with her image, she soon turned out to be incredibly resourceful when it came to getting transportation, finding cheap marijuana, and accessing information about birth control.

Willy observed that if the group of us ever all came together in the same place at the same time, it would make a fascinating tableau. Katy was slightly plump, busty, blond, loud, and daring; she had little patience and let everyone know it. If Katy didn't want to do something, she didn't do it. Conversely, if Katy decided to try something no one else was interested in, she'd go it alone. Cheryl was actually overweight, but had long, dark hair, huge dark eyes, and one hell of a rack. Cheryl's father bought one of the first red Mustangs off the assembly line, and neither of Cheryl's parents were home much, leaving the house wide open for whatever we wanted to do. Cheryl had amazing art skills, and stayed in the background, observing. She never led but was always willing to go along for the ride. Connie was tall and slender like me, with long blond hair and parents willing to offer up their car the minute Connie turned sixteen. Connie didn't display much personality, but had a good heart and a sense of adventure. We had Linda, who was plump with long dark hair and a great personality; she lightened the mood wherever we went. Linda was typically up for anything, and always managed to find something funny about any given situation. I'd introduced sexy (and already sexual) Rita into the group. She had unbelievable guts and great connections. Her mother was divorced and hung out with sailors on shore leave, a fact the rest of us kept hidden from our parents. Aside from occasional visits by Rita's ancient grandmother, their house was often delightfully empty. Rita could be trusted to save your life, but she'd steal the concert tickets right out of your pocket.

Katy and I managed to make friends with Yvette, who was sexually active with real rock stars at fourteen, and who worked alone. Yvette didn't have to smuggle hair color capsules into her apartment; she used her allowance to have her hair dyed Marilyn Monroe platinum at a local salon. She wore lace underwear, which at that time was almost impossible to find. Yvette, who hadn't looked like much in grade school, managed to create a traffic-stopping image. Her breasts bounced and her hips undulated. That platinum hair swayed, and guys oohed and aahed when she explained that her unfashionably fair skin was the result of a moonburn. There were Pam and Sandy, who didn't really hang out with us much, but were part of the network. Pam was short, built, and loud, and Sandy was tall, thin, and funny; both were reliable. There was blond and athletic Vickie, who now went to a different high school but stayed in touch, as did adorably Italian Nina. Our own little Lolita, Cathy Costa, remained part of our network. She put her naturally-blond and innocent look to work by making her up eyes and showing as much cleavage as was legal. The network also included tall, dark Tina Van Voorhees, with her ever-growing connections. Tina didn't smile much, and could bark orders like a Marine sergeant. She paced constantly.

And then there was Jeanne. She had a cute shape and long brown hair, but refused to wear much makeup or hem her skirts appropriately short. She had huge hazel eyes, but her nose was unfortunately bulbous and her mouth almost non-existent. She was attractive, but she never stopped traffic; in fact, she never turned a head. We all vacillated about Jeanne. For a while, early on, she was my closest friend. I knew that beneath the neurosis, Jeanne was a decent person. Although her parents were filthy rich, they accepted me and my lower-middle-class upbringing without question. Jeanne's mother often talked to me about personal things she never brought up with Jeanne. And again, Jeanne's father could pull strings and her mother would drive us anywhere. I loved Jeanne and always felt at home with her family.

Rita and I accidentally created a code. The first rule of that code was initially just between the two of us. If Rita said something completely off the wall, I would immediately back her up and vice versa. Most of these lies were ad-libbed to throw other real rock star chasers off the scent: "You weren't supposed to tell anybody they're staying at the Beverly Hilton!" "I'm sorry! Go get your mom to drive us over there." And, of course, the group in question was staying at the Ambassador or the Beverly Hills.

Over the years new friends came into the group and others disappeared. People moved away, got frightened by the budding counterculture, and went off to school. Some died. Despite disputes, life-altering experiences, and a changing world, several of us stayed in touch, and still do.

Cathi, now part of the group, asked her mother to drive us to the Long Beach Auditorium the day of that first Rolling Stones concert. We arrived two hours before the show. We knew where the band was staying, but had come directly to the auditorium, hoping to see the Stones arrive.

There were several vehicle entrances at the back of the auditorium, but the network had no word on where the Stones would arrive. Some thought the guys were already inside. Jeanne, happy to be at a concert again, walked the sidewalk with me around the auditorium. As we passed one of the back entrances, we heard British accents coming from the second floor. Unwilling to miss an opportunity to get close to a real rock star, I climbed a weathered trellis to the balcony above. The trellis didn't reach to the top of the balcony railing, and my arms just weren't long enough to grasp it and pull myself up. There was, however, a tree next to the railing, and the branch jutting out toward the trellis looked substantial. As I was trying to calculate how to get from the trellis to the tree to the balcony, Jeanne hissed that security guards were coming our way. I clung to the top of the trellis and hissed back that Jeanne should just start walking away. I couldn't look down; I was deathly afraid of heights. As Jeanne's footsteps faded, I heard the security guards laughing. They passed by, apparently never looking up.

From the trellis top, there was a clear view of the balcony, but now I was alone and couldn't decide whether I felt more afraid or stupid. During the half-minute I pondered this, a sliding door opened and an adorable guy with long hair walked out with a tray of paper cups. We locked eyes; he dropped the tray, and ran to my rescue. "No, luv," he instructed with an accent, "just set your right foot on the tree there and I'll give you a lift." I planted my foot on the branch, gave myself a push, and he had me in a bear hug. One painful yank and I was on the balcony, feeling like an absolute jackass. The guy shouted, "We've got a pretty little one here," and two other guys joined us. I waited for laughter, but polite introductions were made all around, as if I'd just shown up for tea. The guy who had rescued me, Jon ("without an 'h'"), asked if I was looking for "the boys." I nodded, again like an absolute jackass, and was told they were about to take the stage. One of the others, an older man who appeared both drunk and amused, offered me souvenirs. I scored a soggy napkin that had been used to mop up Mick's spilled coffee, and a couple of cleaner ones sporting spots of coffee and makeup. Jon handed me several photos, which I tucked in the waistband of my skirt. He looked me over and asked how old I was. I learned what would become the second rule of our code, which was to never give your real age.

When I admitted how young I was, Jon said, "Oh, pity you're so fresh." Then he hesitated, grinned, and asked, "Would you be up for a tumble anyhow?" I knew he was asking for sex, and I was willing, but I didn't have a clue about what to do or say. He must have seen me for the utterly naive kid I was, because he smiled and shook his head. His decision was made. "Maybe it's better if you watch the show." I was both disappointed and relieved, although I loved the look of lust in his eyes. We stepped into each other's space and managed several somewhat steamy kisses before we were joined by three more guys and a middle-aged woman. Jon slung his arm around my shoulder like I was his oldest friend and said, "Sorry you have to go; let me walk you down." It was a good thing I didn't have to exit the way I came, because my knees were weak. A handsome Englishman who worked for the Stones had considered sex with me. I'd accomplished a major feat, and felt both girlishly giddy and invincible at the same time. Jon walked me down a back staircase and gave me a last kiss at the ground-floor exit.

I was alone at the back of the auditorium. There wasn't even a security guard in sight. As I raced around to the front entrance, digging frantically for my ticket, I heard a collective scream go up. The Stones were on stage. I'd missed their entrance. As I squeezed into my seat, Jeanne gave me one of her "mother" looks, but I didn't care. Jeanne had never even been kissed, something most of us experienced in sixth or seventh grade. Once I settled in, I took a careful look around. There was one security guard in the auditorium, and he paced up one aisle and down another. He had nothing to worry about. None of us misbehaved at concerts. Not yet.

When I finally focused on the stage, my jaw dropped. I didn't know who the opening acts had been and didn't care, I just knew that the sexiest man alive was on stage ten rows in front of me, moving in a very un-ballet-like way. I liked it. I watched the security guard pass us, and decided to make a move. Clutching the shoulders of the girl in front of me, I hooked my heels on the ridge at the back of her chair, and stood up, balanced in mid-air. I screamed, "Mick!" as loud as I could. Mick faltered, looked in my direction as I stood suspended in space, and gave a big smile as the girl in front of me jumped up and I crashed through the back of the chair. If you've ever been stuck in a folding chair, you know it takes four teenage girls to help you out. My shins were banged up and would eventually bruise and swell, but for a split second I had Mick Jagger's attention, and that was enough for now.

After the concert, we rushed around back hoping to see the Stones leave, but they'd left the minute they exited the stage. One of the opening acts, then the Fender IV but soon to be the Sons of Adam, was signing autographs and posing for photos. A very young plump girl told me she wanted to meet the tall one, who was apparently the lead singer. I locked eyes with a somewhat older, lanky, long-haired man, wearing ultra-modern wire-framed glasses. He looked smart and sexy and I started walking toward him. Then Jeanne had my arm, attempting to steer me to another musician, also signing autographs. I started to walk with her, when somebody shouted, "Cher!" I knew Sonny and Cher weren't there, so I turned. The tall guy was gesturing to me. I told Jeanne to wait a minute. The guy introduced himself as Joe, and asked if I'd wanted to talk to him. Although I hadn't heard his group play, I told him I thought he was talented and enjoyed the performance. We talked for several minutes and exchanged phone numbers.

I walked back toward Jeanne, who surprisingly didn't give me the "mother" look. Instead, she asked me to get an autograph from one of the other members of the Fender IV. He was shorter, had thick shiny hair, and a baby face, which was just Jeanne's type. So I touched Joe's arm and asked if his friend would sign an auto-graph for my friend, jerking my thumb toward Jeanne. Joe got his band-mate, Mike, to scribble an autograph for Jeanne, and told me he hoped he'd talk to me soon. I couldn't get over how sexy he was, and vowed to myself that if he didn't phone me, I'd call him. The last thing Joe said was, "You're how old?" I felt myself blinking rapidly, and ad-libbed a laugh. "I'm always mistaken for a kid," I grinned, "and that's really kind of flattering!" With that, I took Jeanne's arm and rapidly walked away. Cathi spotted me, and pointed to her watch. We'd used up a precious ten minutes, and Cathi's parents were waiting to drive us home, so we hurried to the Willards' old blue station wagon where Cathi gave me the third degree about Joe.

We'd learned from Cathy Costa that the Stones were staying at the Ambassador Hotel, and Cathi managed to convince her parents to make a stop there before heading home. We found the bungalow immediately. There was a guard planted out front and a couple dozen girls gathered on the sidewalk. Fearless from my adrenalin high, I walked right up to the guard and asked him to tell Mr. Wyman that I was the one who'd sold the songs to Leo, one of the Stones' assistant managers. I chose Bill Wyman because I thought the shadow in the window matched his silhouette.

It was true about the songs. During one of my dozen phone calls made to England from the South High pay telephone, in an attempt to reach someone associated with the Beatles or the

Stones, I'd gotten through to a man named Leo. He'd sounded interested when I told him I was part of a folk duo and that I'd begun writing rock songs as well as folk songs. He'd given me an address, and I'd sent off three songs. Several more long phone calls and a couple of weeks later, and Leo sent a check for the equivalent of fifty dollars. I never did find out if "sweat-soaked barroom brawl" became "gin-soaked barroom queen" in "Honky Tonk Women" as my friends suggested, and it didn't matter. I'd received a courtesy check because, for some reason, over a period of a couple of weeks Leo and I had struck up a minor, long-distance friendship. I figured that right now, at the Ambassador Hotel, it might pay off.

The guard obviously delivered my message, because Bill Wyman stepped out onto the porch and waved me in. I couldn't breathe or feel my legs, but I managed to walk to the porch and greet Bill. He wasn't sure what songs Leo bought, but was courteous enough to meet me. He introduced me to Charlie Watts, who gave me a warm handclasp and world's most charming smile. I didn't see any of the other guys. But for three or four minutes I was in the company of two of the Rolling Stones, and I was thrilled.

It had been a monumental day. I'd necked with a Rolling Stones roadie, seen a terrific concert, been given the name and number of a real rock star, and had actually met two of the Stones. Back at home, I air-dried the coffee-stained napkin from backstage at the auditorium, and carefully tucked the others away. Sometime during the day my half-dozen Stones photos were either lost or nabbed by my friends, but I did have Joe's name and phone number. I knew better than to let too much excitement show around my family, so when my aunt asked me how the concert had been, I said, "Very nice."

Jeanne encouraged me to phone Joe right away. She offered me her own home phone. Her parents had ten-page phone bills full of toll calls, and would never know. Of course, Jeanne made this offer because she wanted to talk to Mike, "the really really cute one," whose autograph she now kept by her bed. But I figured I had nothing to lose, and made the call. I was glad I'd behaved like an adult around Joe, because he told me he was glad I called, and we had a nice conversation about music. I figured I wouldn't have been given that respect if I'd acted like a giggly autograph-hunter the day we met. When I got home, I called Rita, and laid down the third rule of the code, which was to never ask for an autograph. She understood that only teenyboppers asked for signatures, and agreed to the rule.

Joe quickly became my own personal real rock star. The first chance I got, I attended an outdoor afternoon Fender IV concert so I'd understand his music, which was remarkably good. He saw me in the crowd, pointed me out to the rest of the audience, and dedicated a song to me. It was just a small concert at the coast, but Joe made me feel special.

When I wanted to talk to Joe while at home, I could now take the phone into the front bedroom where my grandmother slept. The cord was lengthened when Nana became less mobile, and from her room I could see if Mom was eavesdropping from the hall, one of her favorite pastimes. After Joe's first couple of toll calls to me, I decided it looked childish to lay all the expense on him, so I convinced my mother that a music publisher was interested in my work and that I'd pay for toll calls. She'd seen the check from Leo, and had heard most of what I'd written, so although she grumbled about a rising phone bill, she knew I was good for the money and agreed.

The Dave Clark Five was coming to L.A., and a popular radio station held a contest to determine whether the Dave Clark Five or the Beatles were the best group. It was a silly contest. The Dave Clark Five were obviously cheap Beatle imitators, but we all tuned in for the latest voting tallies. In a long-distance radio interview, Dave Clark expressed a lot of enthusiasm for this contest. His band was being compared to the biggest band to ever hit the planet. We decided the Dave Clark Five were musically acceptable, but they weren't real rock stars. They were soccer players who'd found a way to make some quick money.

Nobody actually wanted to see the band play, but I convinced Jeanne, Connie, Katy, and Cheryl to buy front-row balcony tickets with me. I begged an old white sheet from my grandmother, and painted a sign. We carried it into the concert in my shoulder bag, along with a roll of duct tape. Just before the Dave Clark Five ran on stage, we taped the top edge of the sheet to the railing and let it unfurl. It read "It's Been A Hard Day's Night And You Aren't Helping Any." The on stage security guard must have heard about the contest because he started laughing, and some of the girls on the floor giggled. Most of them booed. Best of all, Dave Clark and his band seemed momentarily distracted by our flag. Jeanne said I had a mean streak, and I told her it was called wit. Besides, the band made a nice chunk of change from our ticket purchases. And, as I'd hoped, our flag was a minor feature photo in the next day's local newspaper, and the radio station holding the Beatles versus the Dave Clark Five contest mentioned our sign, several times, on the air. I phoned the disc jockey and identified myself, and he interviewed me for almost five minutes. The bottom line was we attracted attention, and in those days any attention was good.

The following Friday, Katy spent the night. She'd discovered how to sing in the middle voice, and I'd learned two great guitar pieces from a visiting cousin. Our music was improving, and we had our own gang of groupies at the Pizza Palace and Timmy's. We were too young to audition at any of the actual clubs, so we settled for what we had. We were sure our time would come.

In the morning we pulled on bell-bottoms and crop tops, walked the four miles to Willy's, then headed for Third Street in Hermosa Beach. Katy's latest love interest, Eddie, lived there with his widowed mother. He was only in a garage band, but the band really rocked, and Katy had hopes they'd make it in the business. We spent the day at the beach, in the shade up against the wall where kids hung out to neck. I'd thought through the idea of having sex with Willy because I knew him, I liked him as a person, he was adorable, and he was safe. But as high school kids we didn't have anywhere to go. No respectable parent would allow

their child to entertain a member of the opposite sex in the bedroom, not even in the middle of the day with the door open. We
continued to make out on the beach and in the balcony of the Fox
Theater. Willy was seriously interested in British music and swore
he was going to move to England. He was older than the rest of
us, pushing eighteen, and had no real reason to stay in L.A. One
of Willy's favorite bands, Herman's Hermits, was giving a concert
the following weekend, and Willy and I bought tickets.

The Rose Bowl is bad on the best day. The day of the concert was blistering hot and the arena was jammed with sweaty,
screaming kids. Although we had decent seats, the glare was so
rude we could hardly see. There were some great acts, the Lovin'
Spoonful opened for Herman's Hermits, but I was glad to get home
that night. Willy had talked incessantly about going to England. I
started to think he might actually do it.

The Kinks came into town, and someone in the network let us
know they were staying at the Continental Hotel. Katy, Jeanne,
and I went into Hollywood on Saturday, to find just a few girls
walking the block in front of the hotel. A cop with a bullhorn
kept repeating that no loitering was allowed. The entrance was
guarded. This was a new experience. Security was getting tighter
around real rock stars. A couple of girls asked me for my autograph, something that happened so frequently now, I simply said,
"I'm not Cher."

We walked away from the crowd, around the side of the building, and down the ramp to the valet parking area. We found ourselves in front of a huge garage. The workers inside were wearing
coveralls, performing some kind of maintenance work. The loud-
est of them kept shouting that he was hungry, so we waited. Not
long after noon, the whole group of them retreated to the back of
the garage and we tip-toed in. The entrance to the hotel was wide
open. What was this about? Did security think we were stupid?
We walked in, and went directly to the elevator with house keys
conspicuously between our thumbs and forefingers. From a dis-
tance, a key was a key, and because we were nicely dressed, hotel

personnel didn't bother us. We took the elevator to the top, and then walked around each floor, working our way down. We weren't sure what would tell us which rooms belonged to the Kinks, but we kept going. Because we lacked a specific plan, Jeanne began fussing again. She mentioned her algebra homework. I raised an eyebrow at Katy. Why was Jeanne here?

Several floors down, we spotted three pair of boots setting outside a door, waiting to be picked up and polished. Katy knocked and a short guy with long hair answered. We said we'd met the guys earlier and they'd told us to stop by. Wow, were we surprised.

Inside the Kinks' suite, we found Pam and Sandy, in bed with Dave and Ray. Our coolness dissolved into laughter. Our host popped open bottles of Coke and handed them to Katy and me. We sank into the world's cushiest sofa and discussed rock music for a few minutes, while Pam, Sandy, and their current real rock stars did their thing in the next room, door wide open. With a thank you we left, only to realize Jeanne was gone. We found her in front of the hotel, angry. Katy and I didn't understand what we'd done wrong. Jeanne had chosen to opt out on this venture, and once Katy and I got inside the suite we hadn't stayed long. Jeanne deserted us, not the other way around. I needed to re-establish my relationship priorities so I wasn't hanging out with anyone who'd drag me down.

In an attempt to get our group back on track, I phoned Rita. She was in tears, and Rita didn't cry. My first thought was that her grandmother had died, but no, Rita was pregnant. It wasn't even the mid-sixties, she was barely fourteen, and she was pregnant. Her mother would kill her, and her father, a businessman with very rough edges, would kill her again. Abortion, the obvious solution, was a felony. I had to help Rita.

We accessed the network, and Cathy Costa came through with a name and phone number. The doctor told Rita to come alone with four hundred dollars and avoid the front desk at his motel. Rita was to go straight to his room. Ed willingly offered up the four hundred; at least money wasn't a problem. Rita didn't want to abort this baby but Ed's personal situation wouldn't allow him to take on the role of father or husband. But he was supportive; he wanted to forego his gig to help Rita through the abortion, but the other members of the group gave him hell. So Willy and I drove Rita to the motel and waited in Willy's brother's car the half hour it took for Rita to have the procedure done on a collapsed motel bed by a guy in jeans and a T-shirt, wielding knitting instruments. He was one of the safe ones.

Rita stumbled to the car in terrible pain. I wedged her between Willy and me, and held her tight until we found a local clinic, where she was required by law to give the name of the abortionist. Rita gave the fictitious doctor's name all young girls used then. The character had become so real hospital personnel and the police department knew the name immediately. A D&C cleaned up what the doctor had done, and Rita was put on antibiotics. While she was being tended to, Willy and I were grilled by clinic personnel. We stuck to the story that Rita had phoned us from a motel and asked us to pick her up. When she said she was in pain, we drove her to the clinic. Nobody believed us, but since they couldn't prove anything, they couldn't do anything. We called Ed at the concert hall. He asked us to take Rita home and promised he'd be there as soon as he could.

At Rita's house, we told her mother Rita's period came on suddenly, with a vengeance, and she needed to go to bed. Rita remained undaunted, asking for a washcloth and her makeup case. Willy and I stayed until Ed showed up late afternoon; he snuck in with a bouquet of flowers and a set of four Waterford glasses for Rita's ever-growing hope chest. It was our first abortion.

Rita was younger than me, she was in love, had gone through an abortion, and was collecting items for her future with a wealthy man. I, on the other hand, was still a virgin. It was embarrassing. I just had to choose somebody and get it over with.

The Billy J. Kramer and the Dakotas and Gerry and the Pacemakers double-bill concert was a welcome change of pace. It was like the old days, a whole year earlier. Cathi and Connie had front-row seats, and Cathi squeezed me in between the two of them. Jeanne hung back in the fourth row, not terribly happy. Security was light at this concert, because Billy J. Kramer and Gerry Marsden were nice young British guys, and teenyboppers chased nice guys. Bad boys, like the Kinks, rated higher security. It was as if Pinkerton Security and the Los Angeles Police Department had made it their personal cause to keep us all virgins.

Rita was healing and the two of us had been discussing how to re-group. We would, one way or another, turn things around to our advantage, although our respective priorities were changing. I intended to be involved in music, and Rita had decided to marry well; right now that meant hooking Ed. Secure in the knowledge that I had at least one solidly determined comrade, I felt free to make a jackass of myself at the concert.

My first little trick was to climb on stage by hanging onto Billy's foot with my right hand and his overheated amp with my left. My hand blistered immediately. This was not a good start. Then I noticed the balcony was blocked off halfway around the auditorium. I knew why. I'd heard about this through our faithful network. Cathi said I was doing it again, which meant I was blinking rapidly; it was some weird reaction my eye muscles had to my brain coming up with an idea. It wasn't hard to get into any balcony anymore. Everybody wanted to be on the floor, because it allowed ready access to the stage, and girls were getting bolder. So I walked to the back of the auditorium in the direction of the restrooms, took a turn, and started up to the balcony. Cathi had been watching me, and was soon at my heels. "I know what you're doing," she stated. I shushed her. Security was on the floor, so it was simple to walk along the back row of the balcony. It was only when we got past the barricade and into the light that people began to notice us and cheer us on. Cathi and I were both dancers, and right then we were so glad.

We had to step out over the balcony railing, grasp the top of the curtains, and then climb backward down the rotting fabric onto the stage. The audience was shouting for us, and the band was laughing so hard they could barely sing. We dropped to the floor and ran. I don't remember who I hugged, but I grabbed one of the Dakotas. Cathi nabbed somebody else. One of the security guards was after us, so I decided to get on all fours, backward, and drop off the stage to the ground. I was a split second from freedom when I felt my right leg being pulled, and heard a ripping sound. I landed on my side. A middle-aged woman who had brought her nine-year-old son to the concert decided to take matters into her own hands by physically removing me from the stage.

My knee was screaming and I was madder than hell. Jeanne was next to me, shrieking. The front of my white Mary Quant nylons were torn and my knee was ripped open. Blood trickled down into my shoe. Cathi got to the floor, saw what happened, and yelled for a guard. No one responded. So as the musicians waved to the crowd and exited the stage, Cathi pulled down the entire front stage curtain. I'd seen curtains fall on performances before, but this was unique. The fabric was faded and worn, making it easy for girls to rip it into souvenir pieces. Jeanne was in a shouting match with the woman who'd done the damage to my knee, threatening her with a lawsuit. It was great. I'd never seen Jeanne so impassioned. We ended up leaving quietly, with blisters, open wounds, bloody clothing, and curtain swatches as souvenirs. In the parking lot, Jeanne's mom saw me limping and rushed to help bandage my knee. Jeanne told her father what had happened. She was both enraged and articulate. The most important thing I took away from that concert was a new impression of Jeanne.

On Monday after school I sat on my bed with a steno pad and pen. I'd borrowed my father's ten-inch black-and-white TV so I wouldn't miss *Never Too Young*. I needed to organize my life. Being focused was the only way I got things done, and right now I was living in limbo. One day I was involved in an illegal abortion, and the next day I was performing foolish acrobatics at a concert. But thankfully my social life was entertaining, in significant contrast to my home life. Mom was always drinking, and Nana had begun spouting biblical quotes. No matter how much I moved words and numbers, I couldn't figure out what to do.

A very bright and respected student on the South High campus began to attend war protests. In less than two years, most of our male buddies would be eligible for the draft. Willy was eligible now. Guys were dying over there. We watched them fall every night on the news. Timothy Leary encouraged us to "turn on, tune in, and drop out," and we were enticed by his ideas. After all, he was a brilliant man. Racial tension was on the rise, and my sister and her family lived frighteningly near what would soon be known as the Watts Riots zone. The initial high of the British invasion was fading, and music was taking on a new sound. There was an undercurrent of desperation to everything, and it made us even more anxious to do everything we could to feel alright because it could all end in the blink of an eye.

Joe became the stabilizing force in my life. I talked to him every chance I got. On weekends, he and his buddy Bruce often drove down to the beach. We typically met in a coffee shop, where we got just enough stares to make it miserably impersonal. The Sons of Adam had opened for the Stones and other major bands, and were now playing the Troubadour and the Whiskey (then the Whiskey A Go Go), and their second single was getting a lot of air time. There was just no privacy. Joe decided I should visit him at home in Laurel Canyon.

Some of us had been through driver's ed in school, and the older of us had their learner's permits. Cathi, whose mother was an absolute sweetheart and in very poor health, didn't understand that driving with a learner's permit required a licensed driver over eighteen to be in the car. Cathi became our first real ride, and I'd made the mistake of telling her Joe wanted me to visit. I considered Joe mine, and didn't want unnecessary competition, so when Cathi offered to drive me to Laurel Canyon, I didn't know what to say.

Joe made me safe. Knowing that he wanted me to visit him at home gave me something to hang on to. But Cathi had been interested in him since the Stones concert, and I didn't want to share him.

SECTION TWO
Sex, Drugs, Rock and Roll

Chapter Six

"Mama Told Me Not to Come"
Three Dog Night

athi knew I didn't want her with me at Joe's house. Undaunted, she invited me to a sleepover, promising a special surprise. Gail, a new friend, would be there too. My mother talked to Cathi's mom ahead of time, as usual. Everything was cool. My father dropped me off at Cathi's. Gail arrived within minutes; her parents were on their way out of town overnight. This new friend was short and cute with long brown hair and a great smile. She wasn't full of personality, but I liked her immediately. Cathi's mother was in bed and her father was taking care of the grocery shopping. Gail and I carried our things into Cathi's room, but Cathi told me not to get too comfortable. Gail grinned.

We flipped through the dog-eared parts of *Tropic of Cancer* for about half an hour, keeping quiet at Cathi's request. Once the house was still, Cathi told me to grab my purse and come with her and Gail. She briefly awakened her mother with the news that we were going to Gail's. Mrs. Willard didn't know Gail's parents were gone for the weekend, so she nodded and wished us a good time. Cathi got behind the wheel of the old blue station wagon and the three of us drove off into the night.

On Fourth Street in Hermosa Beach, you could literally smell marijuana in the air. Cathi and Gail had gotten stoned before, but I was new to this. A long-haired guy waved to Cathi from the curb. She pulled over, there was a brief exchange, and we drove off with a four dollar sandwich bag full of weed. Another felony. Being caught with any amount of weed was immediate and serious trouble. We were aware that a teacher at West High had gone to jail for having one tiny marijuana seed stuck to the bottom of his shoe, and Rita knew a guy who had gone to prison for having a small bit of chopped weed on the inside of his lip. We understood the potential necessity of literally eating a joint if cops were in the vicinity. Yet here we were with an entire bag of the stuff, and Cathi was driving without a license. Amazingly, we made it back to Gail's house, where we started making phone calls. Cathi ran to the corner market for sodas and munchies. Gail's parents had cutting-edge color TV, and we had a bag of weed. We were going to have a party.

By 10:30 there were ten or twelve people at Gail's place. Two guys from a new L.A. band showed up, as did a reporter from an underground newspaper. Gail, Cathi, and I were the only girls, and all the guys were older. Most of them were interesting.

We used Gail's father's favorite pipe. Cathi took me aside and told me how to smoke dope. She didn't want me making an ass of myself, and neither did I. The pipe was passed counterclockwise around the circle on the living room floor. When it was handed to me, I did as Cathi had instructed, and exhaled my first lungful of weed successfully. Once we'd decided we'd all had enough, Gail demanded our attention with several sharp taps on her Coke bottle. She'd waited until we were loaded to announce that her father was a detective for the Los Angeles Sheriff's Department, and we'd just smoked dope from his favorite pipe.

When the laughter died down, I realized things looked brighter. Gail's mother had a collection of colored glass vases on the windowsill that utterly hypnotized me. Someone brought me out of my reverie by suggesting a game of Clue, which seemed like a remarkably intelligent idea. After about two rounds, I realized nobody was hiding their score pads; all the information I needed was right there in front of me. So I spent the next couple of hours cheating and winning big at Clue.

Al, the reporter, herded us into the TV room to check out the late-night movie, starring Peter Lorre. After somebody passed the pipe again, we came to the group consensus that Peter Lorre's eyes had some magical quality, and they were hysterically funny.

When the movie was over and the National Anthem played, the TV screen showed early a.m. fuzz. None of the channels would broadcast again until morning. Cathi backed a dark-haired hunk into one bedroom; Al took a staggering Gail by the hand, and I ended up in the TV room with an overly-attentive guy named Matthew. I'd been flirting with one of the musicians, but Matthew flatly stated I was with him and the musician politely backed off. When I couldn't take any more of Matthew's attempts at groping, I drifted back into the living room where a couple of guys were talking and everyone else was sleeping. I grabbed a throw pillow from the sofa, lay down on the floor, and fell asleep.

The next morning, we cleaned up the house and washed dishes, taking special care with the pipe. We opened all the windows to air out the house. One by one the guys left. When we three girls were alone, Gail freaked out. She thought she'd had sex with Al, but she wasn't sure. She liked him, and he wanted to see her again, so it was decided he was an acceptable first-timer. We showered, applied eyeliner and mascara, got into bell-bottoms and shirts, and drove back to Cathi's house. When my mother half heartedly asked how it had gone, I told her we'd watched a movie.

Chapter Seven

"Young Girl, Get Out of My Mind"
Gary Puckett and the Union Gap

Cathi had succeeded. I felt indebted to her for introducing me to weed. Saturday we were going to visit Joe in Laurel Canyon.

On Friday night Sonny and Cher played the Rev. Rita made sure that Katy, Eddie, Willy, and I were at the front of the stage. When Sonny walked out, he looked at me, did a double-take, and said, "Wow." When Cher sang solo, she stood right in front of us. Willy was drooling. "Look at her," he kept whispering, in awe. I wanted to kick him and say, "Hey! Look over here, jackass! See a resemblance?" I left the stage before Sonny and Cher were done with their performance and the Turtles took the stage.

It was soon 10:00, Rev curfew time. Someone's parents were always there by 10:15 to pick us up. I wasn't allowed to stay out after dark unless I was babysitting, sleeping over with a friend, or at the Rev. Mark of the Turtles tried to convince me to go home with him that night, and I was tempted. After several minutes of serious thought, I chose to jump in Connie's mom's car and go home. I remembered the hell my sister suffered for simply coming home shortly after her curfew. If I risked staying out all night, my mother's wrath would be unbearable. Besides, I'd been half-naked with Mark, and he just wasn't the one. I needed to lose this nagging virginity, but I hoped it would be with Joe.

Cathi picked me up the next morning and steered the old blue station wagon onto the freeway. Halfway to Laurel Canyon, Cathi pulled out a joint. Was she nuts? Nobody smoked dope on the L.A. freeway in broad daylight! We could go to jail! But Cathi wanted to show up loaded, so we took our chances.

At the house, Joe gave me a wink and a grin, nodded to Cathi, and introduced us to a couple members of Love, who were hanging out for the day. They seemed like good people. I was glad to see that Mike, Joe's fellow band member and roommate, was there too. I hoped he'd keep Cathi busy. I heard other voices coming from the back of the house; a guy and girl were giggling, and two men were holding a disagreement. Someone else was playing the same guitar piece over and over. Then I heard a louder feminine voice. An older girl was in the kitchen, making spaghetti from scratch "for Joe and the boys." My heart sank. From the bad dye job, the cheap earrings, the almost non-existent clothes, and the way she looked at Joe, I knew what she really wanted. Everybody there knew what she wanted. I suddenly felt young and foolish, and would have been satisfied to say we'd just stopped in to say hello, gotten back into the old blue station wagon and left, but Cathi was already settled down in front of the TV, with her upper torso draped across Joe's thighs. I wanted to kill her. After that first meeting with Joe, all the phone conversations, and the visits with Joe and Bruce, I'd come with an intention in mind. I could stand to temporarily lose Joe to an experienced groupie like Kitchen Girl, but not to Cathi. I needed my own transportation, even if I had to drive illegally like Cathi did. I should have followed my instincts and kept her away from Joe. It wasn't even noon, and the day had gone to hell. Cathi had, within two or three minutes, already made a move on Joe, and he apparently just wanted me to hang out while the aging tart in the kitchen cooked dinner for him. I had been geared up for first-time sex with Joe, and ended up watching TV. I was beyond disappointed; I had a nagging feeling something was very wrong.

Discouraged by Joe but determined to lose my virginity, I considered asking Ken of Love if he wanted to have sex. I'd heard from Yvette that real groupies didn't hesitate to offer themselves to real rock stars. Ken had cuddled up next to me on Joe's lounge, and eventually slung his arm around me. I didn't think delivering a proposition would be a faux pas. Ken and I talked, and he began teasing me. I touched my finger to his mouth, and he grinned and bit my fingertip, so I told him I was going into the other room. Ken got up with me, but as soon as I headed for the hall, Joe was on his feet and had me by my upper arms. Out of the corner of my eye, I could see Ken back into the living room, and suddenly I was just a kid again. I fell all over myself apologizing for having shown up on a day Joe had a dinner date. He just laughed. Then he picked me up and carried me into his bedroom.

Joe laid me on the bed and pulled the curtains. Despite a twinge of fear, this was exactly what I'd wanted. But now that it was happening, I couldn't think of anything to do or say.

We kissed for a long time. They were emotionally-charged kisses that came from my heart. It was the first time I felt adult love for a man. Joe started to reach under my top, but caught himself. He kissed my stomach, then sat up and looked at me. "We can't, you know." Suddenly I was angry. I'd known something was wrong. He saw the look on my face. I sat up and asked what was stopping us. "I know how old you are," he said. "Cathi told me." I can't even spell the obscenities that went through my head.

In the mid-sixties, statutory rape was a felony and I already knew that two of Joe's acquaintances had gone to jail for it. Joe was smart; he wasn't taking any chances and I couldn't blame him. I wasn't mad at Joe, but Cathi was another matter. After Joe and I bemoaned our fate for awhile, we got dressed and went to Wallach's Music City. We bought the strings he needed, and he introduced me to the people there as his girl.

When we got back to the house, everybody was watching the popular music show, *It's Boss*. Joe obviously hadn't seen it before, because he asked what was on TV, and everybody said *It's Boss*. Joe agreed that yes, it looked boss, but what show was it? Again, myself included this time, everybody said *It's Boss*. It took a solid five minutes to untangle Joe's mind enough to explain that the name of this boss show was *It's Boss*.

Joe answered a call from Kitchen Girl, and Ken came over to me, nuzzled his head into my neck in a goofy way that made me smile, and said, "Next time for sure." We grinned and tickled each other. "Deal?" he whispered, and I hissed, "Deal."

Ken asked if I'd been on tour with Joe, and I explained that I'd never been on tour with anyone. Traveling of any kind frightened me. I had no sense of direction, and I got a nasty feeling of utter disorientation in unfamiliar places, like I had in Las Vegas. Ken seriously considered what I said and told me I might try just touring the West Coast, possibly with a well-organized band that stuck to a specific schedule. He tossed out the idea of me taking a trip to a San Francisco gig with Love. That sent my head spinning. I didn't want this beautiful creature to know my age, and he honestly seemed sincere. Ken was apparently aware that I was uneasy, and told me to think about it. He gave me a phone number and told me to stash it away. He didn't want to create any problems with Joe. He seemed to think Joe and I had an ongoing sexual relationship, which made me want to laugh and cry at the same time. I promised I'd think about a West Coast trip.

When the TV show was over, Cathi said we'd better leave for home. Although she knew I'd been in Joe's bedroom with him, she'd spent the rest of afternoon hanging on him. I'd soon learn that Cathi made a habit of going after other girls' men, but that understanding didn't make her behavior any easier to take. Joe continued giving me smiles, but he didn't bother to extract himself from Cathi, even when she began moving in on his thighs again. My teeth were clamped together so hard my head hurt, and halfway home I realized I had a bloody palm from clenching my right fist. I leapt out of the car before it came to a complete stop, and left Cathi with the words, "Remember who your real friends are." Those words would return to haunt both of us time and again.

Later, I realized I'd lost Ken's phone number. I checked the curb where Cathi had dropped me off, and the next day when Cathi phoned, sounding innocent as could be, I told her to search the station wagon. The scrap of paper was gone, so Cathi suggested I get the number from Joe. Ken would have made a terrific first sexual partner, but if I took Cathi's advice, Joe might think I preferred Ken to him. I couldn't take that chance. I loved Joe.

On Monday at school, Yvette, who had already slept with Michael of the Byrds, a handful of roadies, and was currently sleeping with Neil Young, confided to Katy and me that over the weekend, Neil told her if he was ready to settle down, he'd ask her to marry him. Neil Young was big time, he was in love with one of us, and I hadn't even gotten laid yet.

Rita was still sleeping with Ed of the Turtles, Katy was with Eddie, Connie was spending nights with Limey of Limey and the Yanks, Cathi had hooked up with a cute guy from San Pedro High, and Yvette had Neil Young. I wasn't sure about Cheryl or Linda, but I did know about Cathy Costa. I'd seen her in a popular teen magazine with Freddie of Freddie and the Dreamers, and given her a call. She was screwing everybody. The network was in tact, but our friendships were on shaky ground because those who were sexually active had a hard time relating to those of us who weren't. I was still so mad at Cathi I could have choked her.

In search of a drastic change of pace, I phoned Jeanne. Pure, innocent Jeanne, who was saving herself for marriage unless Paul McCartney came through. We all figured Paul wasn't going to show up on her doorstep, and that, for her, marriage was a long way off. Jeanne had run into Tina Van Voorhees downtown, and Tina said her aunt had ushered a number of British rock stars into celebrity holding at the airport over the past week. Tina didn't have names, but confessed the guys had been under top security. This news coincided with radio information that someone important was staying in the home of a famous family in Benedict Canyon. Jeanne's mother had agreed to drop her off in the canyon on Saturday, but Carol was busy and Debbie wasn't interested. Did I want to come along? At first I said no. I didn't want to traipse around the canyon in this unseasonably hot weather with Jeanne, who claimed to want to meet real rock stars but never followed through on a plan. But I was curious about who was in town. Rita didn't have any information but would try to track down her uncle, so I phoned Cathy Costa. She told me one radio station insisted all four of the Beatles were here, and our other favorite station said the Stones were in town. Apparently somebody was hidden away in Benedict Canyon, so I phoned Jeanne back and said I'd go. If nobody wanted to have sex with me, I might as well get a good sunburn. Anything was better than watching Mom stagger around the house cursing under her breath.

Chapter Eight

"(K)nights in White Satin"
The Moody Blues

Southern California does not have seasons. We have cold (under 75 degrees), warm (75 to 85 degrees), hot (85 degrees and up), and Santa Ana conditions (still, dry, and over 100 degrees). Saturday we were having an unseasonal Santa Ana. I washed and steam ironed my hair, did my best Cher makeup job, and put on flowered bell-bottoms and a short yellow top. I added hoop earrings and sandals, and was ready to go.

I felt oddly uncomfortable riding in the car with Jeanne and her mother. I hadn't made much progress in my attempt to become a groupie. What was I doing wrong? Was Jeanne's non-negotiable virginity wearing off on me? Maybe it was contagious; we'd spent a lot of time together. Jeanne's mother dropped us off in front of a Benedict Canyon mansion with a gawking audience of about a hundred girls.

This was worse than drifting through hotels looking for real rock stars, because we weren't sure who, if anybody, was here, and in the hills we didn't have access to restrooms, water, or even a pay phone. We asked around, and most of the girls said one radio station had announced a couple of the Beatles were in town.

Others said a couple of the Stones were in town; it was the same information we'd heard before. A very excited chubby little girl insisted the Dubloons were here. Nobody else had ever heard of them, but this kid was about to have a stroke over the idea they might be in the vicinity. Several girls asked for my autograph. One was so pushy ("Oh, you think you're so cool!") that I scribbled my own name and handed the paper back to her. I felt like a jerk. We were baking in the sun in front of some stranger's house on the off chance there was somebody interesting inside. I was still angry at Cathi, and now mad at myself for coming on this wild goose chase with Jeanne.

We were in direct sunlight in front of the house, and my face was starting to sting, so I began walking down the hill where the trees grew together over the narrow street, providing temporary shade. There was no way to get to the house from the front because there were cops everywhere. After all, this was Benedict Canyon. A twenty-minute walk took me, and eventually Jeanne, to the hill behind the house. There were "Beware of Snakes" signs posted, but I'd grown up around snakes and wasn't concerned. Several other girls joined us, mostly younger girls who looked maybe twelve or thirteen. After about ten minutes of smiling politely at "You look just like Cher," "I bet you met somebody really famous already," and "You're lucky your mom lets you wear makeup," I made a decision. We were stuck here until Jeanne's mother picked us up at 4:00, so I'd spend some time climbing the hill and looking for a backyard. A couple of the younger girls followed me up the first part of the slope. I reached the top and found a sign that read "Restricted Entry." Just as I started to climb the chain link fence, a cop with a bullhorn shouted us down. I thought maybe I was safe, that he hadn't seen me, but of course my yellow clothes were a dead giveaway even through thick foliage. The cop climbed up and dragged me down by my ankle.

Jeanne was upset and wanted to walk to the front again to see if she could get some kind of view into the backyard. I let her go. The other girls had been frightened by the cop, and they followed

Jeanne. Blissfully alone, I climbed to the top of the snake-free hill again, and reached the chain link fence. It was only about six feet high, so I climbed it and dropped down on the other side. About twenty yards ahead was a wooden fence, and beyond that was the house.

A wave of fear struck me. Worse, I felt stupid. Hadn't I progressed beyond this sort of thing? As I began to turn back, I heard laughter. I crept up to the wooden fence. It was about ten feet tall and varnished to a high sheen. I could hear splashes; it sounded as if people were getting in and out of a pool. And then I heard a British accent. It wasn't familiar, but it was British. I'd always lacked a reasonable sense of direction, and had no clue as to the layout of this property, so I followed the fence around to the right until I saw a gate. There was now more than one British voice, and all seemed to be male. I dusted myself off, ran my fingers through my hair, and knocked.

A blond guy who looked and sounded like a California surfer opened the gate. He frowned and I thought *Oh damn*. If I ended up in jail for trespassing, my mother would kill me. Surfer Boy asked my name, and I told him I was Sally, known by some as Sunny. I said that (Rita's uncle) told me he was coming by to talk to the guys, and that I should stop by, as if everybody visited by sneaking up to people's back gates. The guy told me (Rita's uncle) wasn't there, then turned around and asked if anybody knew a Sally. Somebody shouted, "I do!" and asked what I looked like. Within about a minute, three dripping wet guys stood staring at me. I didn't know them, and they didn't know me. But one smiled, and with a charming accent said, "It's a wisp of a thing. She looks a little like the pop singer, don't you think? Have her in." And he made a swooping bow to let me know it was all right to enter the backyard.

The place was huge, with an Olympic-size pool, lawn furniture straight out of the Taj Mahal, hand-painted tile, and landscaping that put even Jeanne's mother's award-winning garden to shame. I'd never seen anything like it in my life. There were several guys hanging out, some with British accents and some with a standard California twang. I didn't recognize a single one of them. Oh dear God, what stupid thing had I done now? Surfer Boy asked me why I hadn't used the front door. I had to think fast because time had stopped and I wasn't answering the question. Finally I laughed. "Have you seen the girls out there? You can't even see the door!" The guys smiled and nodded.

Davy, the Englishman who'd allowed me entrance, asked if I'd like something to drink. Although liquor wasn't popular mid-sixties, there were several wine glasses on the tile around the pool. I remembered the fourth rule of our code. When faced with unwanted alcohol, ask for tonic and lemon. Tonic water was always available, and lemon kept your breath fresh. My cheeks were really stinging, and Surfer Boy noticed it. "You're not a native, are you?" he smirked. I told him I certainly was, but that I typically only came out at night. That got a laugh and an "oooh" from the Englishmen and a scowl from Surfer Boy. Davy had stopped and turned back toward me. After a second look at my face and arms, he told me to come inside; he'd look for a bottle of suntan lotion.

My entire family could have lived in that kitchen. Everything was sleek, modern, and insanely clean. The air conditioning felt wonderful. It didn't produce that nasty blast of icy air we used to get when entering air-conditioned buildings. There were several bottles of liquor on one counter, and I watched as Davy poured Schwepp's from a large bottle, then dropped in a slice of lemon and a handful of ice cubes. I noticed a man backlit by the window at the other end of the kitchen, studying the contents of a cupboard. He had long, golden blond hair, and was wearing jeans with an unbuttoned white satin poet's shirt. With no belt or shoes, he appeared very casual. Davy caught my eye and said, "Oh, I'm sorry. Sally, this is Brian. Brian, this is Sally. Or do you know each other?" I dumbly shook my head, then caught myself and greeted Brian with a Trojan attempt at credibility. "I've met Bill and Charlie, and did some work for Leo. Oh, and I know your roadie Jon, but I don't think we've met." I was dusty, sunburned, and terrified, but I had to appear cool. After all, I was staring at the one Rolling Stone the fans of more than one teen magazine voted the cutest guy in rock and roll. He was staring back.

Then he spoke. "You've got a real burn." What kind of greeting was that, and how was I supposed to respond? He came closer. "Your cheeks look like they might blister." He was staring at the red stripe across my face. This was a situation I hadn't dealt with before. One of the elite was showing concern about my health. What was the cool thing to do?

Davy set down a bottle of Coppertone, gave me a pat on the back and gestured that he was going back outside. Brian still looked concerned. He reached out his hand, and I grasped it. We walked down a cathedral-like hall into the largest bathroom I'd ever seen. Brian raided a medicine cabinet the size of my clothes closet, and decided on a tube of some kind of cream. So there I stood, in some unknown person's bathroom, with one of the Rolling Stones putting medicine on my sunburn.

When Brian decided I was going to live, he laid the cream on the counter and slipped his arms around my waist. I returned the gesture by sliding my arms around his neck. The fifth rule of our code was to never question what a real rock star wants to do, just go along with it. He studied my face again, then tipped his head back and said, "You're prettier than she is, you know." I didn't know who "she" was, so I just smiled. Brian ran a hand down my back, over my hip, and around the back of my thigh. He kept staring. Then he let go completely and told me to continue down the hall to the third door on the left. I followed his instructions. Standing outside the door, I could hear voices. They didn't come blaring through the walls like at home; these were pleasantly muffled. A man was singing an unfamiliar song, two other males were holding a conversation, and from behind me I could hear a woman laughing loudly and intermittently as if listening to a comic act. The house was full, yet this particular hall was empty.

Within a couple of minutes, Brian, with my drink and his wine glass between his fingers, joined me in an all-white bedroom. It was cutting-edge chic, the only imperfection being the imprint of a body on the bedspread and pillow.

Slowly, and with very little talking, Brian became my first. A long, lazy hour later, I realized it was getting late, and said I had to go before traffic got too bad on the freeway. Brian gave me that famous shy smile, nodded, and led me through this maze of a house to the front door. He made me promise to take care of my sunburn, and then placed me in the care of a police officer, who asked me where I'd parked. I told him I was meeting a friend up the street, so the cop escorted me to the sidewalk and wished me well. The cop watched me walk away from the crowd; the girls out front quieted down and let me pass. For about two minutes, I was important.

I didn't tell Jeanne. She'd been waiting in the shade and knew something had happened because I'd been gone for hours. The experience had been spontaneous and special, and I wanted to keep it to myself. It was so unlike I expected it would be. It wasn't childlike necking, like with Willy. It wasn't frantic groping, like with Mark. It wasn't star-crossed making out, like with Joe. It was easy and pleasantly surreal. I'd lost my virginity to a real rock star. I felt like a groupie.

Chapter Nine

"Hot Town, Summer in the City"
The Lovin' Spoonful

I turned sixteen in early June at the end of sophomore year. Katy, Linda, and Connie were already sixteen, and Connie had both her driver's license and access to her mother's car. Despite the fact that my own mother had forbidden me to drive until I left home, Connie drove me to the Department of Motor Vehicles, handed me her car keys, and waited while I took the driving test. I'd given my sister's address, so my driver's license wouldn't show up in my parents' mailbox. My mother's drinking had gotten worse, and I lived in terror of her.

One morning I found a nasty run in one of my nylons and was rushing to get ready for school. I shouted to my mother that I needed to borrow a stocking, but she didn't answer. My father and aunt were at work, and I could hear my grandmother in her room, on the telephone. Not knowing what else to do, I went into my parents' room to retrieve a stocking from my mother's drawer. I spotted the right color, gave a tug, and found an envelope snagged to the stocking. It was a letter I'd written to a friend, the envelope ripped open, and the contents obviously read. I dug further in the drawer and came away with an entire stash of letters I'd put out for the mailman to pick up, along with a dozen letters sent to me. The entire stack had been opened.

Less than a week after my discovery, I came home from school, spilled my books and purse on the table, and rushed to the bathroom. Returning two minutes later, I found Mom reading a note she'd taken from the inside zipper pocket of my purse. It mentioned a phone conversation I'd had with Joe, and how he'd sung "Time Is on My Side" while sipping wine. My mother emptied the entire contents of my oversized purse, ripped out the lining, and then went through every one of my schoolbooks. With that note in a very shaky hand, she phoned Jeanne's mother. Although Mom knew Joe was interested in my music, he'd bought several songs from me and set the lyrics to his own melodies, she was furious that I'd had a phone conversation with him when he was sipping wine. Jeanne's mother didn't join in my mother's rage, however, which just further angered Mom.

When my driver's license arrived at Ann's, I stashed it, along with some cash, under the insole of my right boot. My mother now consistently went through pockets and purse, and she inspected my room with a fine-tooth comb, but she never seemed concerned with my footwear because I kept it clean. She didn't even like my boots, so they seemed like the logical hiding place.

It hadn't been long since my encounter with Brian, and everybody knew I'd "done it," just not with who. Rita's uncle knew which musicians visited Los Angeles, even overnight, and one day at lunch she said she knew my secret. It was almost impossible to get anything past Rita, and I wasn't yet ready to give up that beautifully personal experience to my friends. Katy, Connie, and Cheryl gathered to hear the news, but Cathi, loud and insulting as always, declared to the group, "Oh, she was up in the canyons and met some guy." I didn't dispute the comment, and noticed Rita studying my face. She wasn't going to tell. My secret was safe for a while longer.

Now that I'd been de-virginized, I felt obligated to work on really being a groupie. Getting close to the guys who made the music still seemed like the most direct route to making music myself. The Leaves were popular at the time with two different versions of their remarkable hit "Hey Joe." They performed on *Shivaree*, and I made sure I was chosen to be on stage again. During a break, I simply walked backstage and met the band. I ended up spending a couple of wild hours with a member of the group, a guy I could have really fallen for. Another evening I had an unexpected encounter with a member of Quicksilver Messenger Service, who played a couple of gigs with Joe and The Sons of Adam. Joe found out and gave me a lecture about being careful until I was eighteen. I couldn't tell if he was concerned about me or his fellow musicians. The industry was almost incestuous and would only get tighter. One afternoon at a Laurel Canyon hangout called the Garage, I was taken by the hand by Sky of the Seeds. ("You're coming with me, girl.") I didn't go. It was the only time I turned down a real rock star. The Seeds had started out as a garage band in my neighborhood, and played a standing weekend gig at a local piano bar long before becoming a major group with a raft of hits. There was plenty I didn't like about Sky long before we met in a potentially intimate setting.

None of us knew what to do about birth control. The pill wasn't available in the U.S. yet. Diaphragms, I.U.D.s, and other devices were only available to adults. Guys didn't bother to carry condoms, and were insulted if asked to use one; girls were responsible for what happened to their own bodies. We'd never heard of herpes, much less AIDS, so everyone felt relatively safe, except when it came to the problem of pregnancy. We'd heard about homemade Vaseline plugs and other crude sperm-blocking methods, but they were messy and put a crimp in spontaneity.

Cathi screwed up the courage to talk to a college-age neighbor, a girl with a long and colorful reputation. Standard practice in those days was to douche after sex, but we couldn't carry hideously large and bulky douche equipment with us. We knew better than to try to keep it at home, either. Yvette's mother had caught her tending to things one day in the bath. That incident raised a lot of unanswerable questions, even from Yvette's incredibly cool mom. Cathi's friend told us to each always carry a bottle of Coke, Pepsi, or Seven-Up. After sex we were to quickly find a bathroom, uncap the bottles, put our thumbs over the openings, shake up our bottles, and then quickly insert the openings into our vaginas. It created a sticky mess, but the explosion of fizz seemed to work as a makeshift douche. From then on, we all kept Cokes in our shoulder bags.

Statutory rape and related issues were getting more serious. A couple of guys from a major rock group had been caught partying with three completely nude underage girls, and although no sex was involved and no illegal drugs were found, the whole group went to jail. I don't know if this no-nudity thing was actually some new law or just an attempt to rattle the cages of those who wanted to sleep with underage girls. Legal or not, guys were getting busted left and right, and everybody was scared. We heard from Tina Van Voorhees that some girls were wearing strips of cloth tied around their ankles so they wouldn't be considered completely nude in case of a bust. Other girls kept their shoes on, which started a temporary sexy-shoe craze and inspired me to get a pair of spike-heeled boots. In gym class we were shown a film in which a young girl cried that they shouldn't take her boyfriend to jail because they had sex with their shirts on. There were a couple of public protests, but they ended in busts, too. We were in a catch-22. Parents, neighbors, and cops were determined to stop consensual sex among underage girls and potential partners.

The group of us was afraid to wear ankle bands, because we were required to wear dresses to school and many other public places, and a three-inch-wide piece of cloth would provoke questions we wouldn't be willing to answer. So Rita, Cathi, and I met at Cathi's. All girls had a required minimum of home economic classes, so we all knew how to sew. We were sure we could come up with something that could be passed off as merely fashion. Rita got the idea to create a thick thigh garter, so we ran off a prototype on Cathi's machine. It was about four inches wide, had elastic inside, and in a pinch was even sturdy enough to hold up a stocking. We started making our thigh bands in cool-looking fabric, and passed them around to Connie, Cheryl, Katy, and anybody else who asked for them.

Our favorite disc jockey announced the Beatles were coming back to L.A. at the end of summer. Although the concert was a long way off, word already had it they would play at Dodger Stadium and that they'd enter the field via helicopter. If so, there would be no way to meet them. Jeanne was planning to buy tickets but I wasn't sure I wanted to go with her. She'd cut her mousey-brown hair chin length in a modified Vidal Sassoon style, but with her lack of general style, she looked like a bank teller. Her father had, years earlier, decided Jeanne was going to be a lawyer, so her summer would be tied up taking special college classes that would go toward her high school college-prep credits. Although she wasn't one of us anymore, I felt a loyalty to her. I agreed to go on her Beatles ticket list, along with Carol, Debbie, and other people I had nothing in common with.

The Turtles had made it bigger than expected with a couple of commissioned bubblegum songs, and were often on tour, so Rita wasn't seeing much of Ed. Their two-year star-crossed romance suddenly became a case of out of sight out of mind, and Rita was now in competition with the rest of us for the attention of real rock stars. One day she asked me if I wanted to go to the Canyon with her, and I agreed. I assumed we were doing an old-fashioned bus trip. But after meeting at her place, we walked to an office building a couple of blocks away. Rita asked to speak with Mr. So-and-So, who showed up a couple of minutes later in a three-piece suite, all smiles. He gave Rita a remarkably steamy kiss and asked if she was free the next Friday night. Once we left the building, Rita displayed a set of car keys. She still hadn't turned fifteen and didn't even have a learner's permit, but she'd lifted keys from this guy. Rita assured me he was locked in at work all day and wouldn't miss his car, which, to my horror, turned out to be a new Jag.

Although I had a legitimate driver's license, I wasn't about to drive a stolen car, but Rita didn't hesitate to get behind the wheel. We made the trip to Laurel Canyon with Rita struggling to keep the Jag in gear and me continually bitching that we were either going to completely lose the transmission or end up in jail for grand theft auto.

I was surprised Rita didn't stop at Joe's. Instead, she pulled into a curving driveway in front of what appeared to be a castle. A completely plowed girl with long disheveled blond hair was sitting in the sun downstairs. She wanted to hug me, so I held her for a few minutes. Looking up at me, she smiled, said, "You're pretty," and kissed me. After telling me she loved me, she passed out, gently, quietly, on the porch swing. She was wearing a crop top and blue jeans. I'd noticed more and more Canyon girls in jeans and liked the look. Rita shouted for me to come upstairs.

Inside the main room, I recognized an unpleasantly stoned actor from late-fifties TV, and a tall, tanned, blond guy with hair as long as mine. I'd heard about Tanden. He was the only person anyone knew, other than Rodney Bingenheimer, who was trying to make a name for himself on image alone. He was wearing a disgusting amount of glitz and pranced around in the sunlight showing it off. Rita left me with the verbally abusive actor and disappeared into the bedroom with Tanden. Sometimes I hated Rita. She was always pulling things on me, expecting me to have the patience of Job. At least I had the forethought to keep a driver's license and emergency money in my boot. Just as I was about to split, Rita reappeared. As we were leaving, Tanden grabbed Rita and pointed at me. "I want her," he stated. Rita explained that we had to go, but that she'd bring me back later. I hoped I'd never see him again. The image of wealth didn't impress me the way it did Rita. In some ways we were so very different.

Rita took a couple of turns, then doubled back and stopped at the Royal Toilet, an unfenced cliff overlooking much of the

Canyon, Jim Morrison's house specifically. The cliff served as an emergency rest stop for guys, and the bushes gave girls a reasonably private place to pee, if desperate. A couple of guys pulled up behind us. We asked them if they needed private use of the facilities, but they said no, they were just hanging out. I was standing at the edge of the cliff, masochistically testing my fear of heights, when one of the guys grabbed me and lifted me up, over the edge of the cliff. "Look at this tiny waist!" he shouted. I couldn't scream because I couldn't breathe. Several seconds later I was back on solid ground, shaking but relatively safe. Rita did need to use the facilities, even though she'd just been in a bathroom. We figured she had a bladder infection. A couple of weeks later, we'd learn she had gonorrhea.

Right then, I wished I were in bed with a real rock star, one of the guys who made the music that made everything better. I would have settled for pursuing my latest passion, electric guitar. I was working like crazy to buy one of my own, but they were pricey. Rita was annoying me, and I desperately wanted to be doing something else.

After a few more frightening turns, we pulled up onto a patch of gravel. Loud rock music was coming from a garage attached to a small back house. I opened my mouth to ask where we were when I realized it was the Garage, which looked different in the bright light of day. The Garage belonged to a music producer and was a mutual gathering place for musicians. I wondered if Rita was going to leave me with another obnoxious has-been while she had a good time with somebody else. She motioned me out of the car, and we walked to the front door. A pretty dark-haired woman told us to go ahead and use the side door to the garage. Rita opened the door and, after a brief exchange with someone, took me by the arm and pulled me inside. There was a bright light in the corner, but the rest of the space was dark and suddenly quiet. I heard a familiar voice and realized who Rita was talking to about three seconds before I saw Johnny Barbata, the finest drummer to ever work with the Turtles and a legend of his own making.

I never really got to know Johnny during rehearsals at the Rev, but he recognized me. He smiled and told me my hair was very cool now that it was hip-length. And although he was a drummer, he liked the fact that, as just one of a million girls who claimed to play guitar, I could actually produce music. He handed me an electric twelve-string so incredible I thought it should be mounted on a wall and prayed to. I looked at electric twelve-strings the way other people looked at ten-carat diamonds or designer sports cars. Johnny asked me to name a favorite guitar riff, and I told him I liked the Beatles' version of "Words of Love." Nobody there was playing Beatle music, but a couple of guys got together and helped me work it out. The dark-haired woman brought us munchies. It was a welcoming place, and I felt comfortable for the first time all day. Frank Zappa's would become the place to hang out in another couple of years, but then we had the Garage.

Rita got us back to the beach alive. We re-set the odometer on the car so her friend wouldn't question his mileage, and Rita managed to return the car keys. I had to forgive her. After all, I'd gotten to play that electric twelve-string. And the guys at the Garage had invited me back.

The sixth and last agreed upon rule of our code was to avoid hitchhiking. Cops hassled girls who hitchhiked. A lot of runaways were coming to L.A., and although I now had a valid I.D., I was underage and didn't need the grief. So when Rita suggested we start hitching, I made myself scarce. I decided to spend some time making money with Cathi and Gail.

As soon as school was out for the year, the three of us got jobs with a holiday decoration manufacturer in Hermosa Beach. All we had to do was twist things together in an appropriately aesthetic way. And we could sit and talk while working. The place was run by an enterprising long-hair who didn't care much about clock time as long as the work got done.

That first weekend, Gail threw another sleepover. This time, however, one of the guys pulled out a piece of waxed paper with little raised pink dots on it. It was acid, at five dollars a tab. I didn't know what to do about the temptation to try serious drugs. I'd watched mere alcohol turn my once tolerable mother into a beast; to this day I can't stand the combined smell of perfume, cigarette smoke, and liquor. Weed and hash seemed safe, but acid was a different animal. Then again, I'd always been willing to try anything once. I asked Cathi and Gail what they thought. Cathi flatly said I wasn't stable enough for hallucinogenics and that I wouldn't be able to handle LSD. Cathi wasn't even willing to try it herself yet. Gail, always grounded and amazingly pragmatic, decided to go for it. Two hours into her first trip, she said it was just another nice high.

It was a hot day in August when my mother shouted from her bedroom, and my mother didn't shout; she preferred to use stony silence for effect. The Watts Riots were raging, and my sister lived too near for comfort. Mom had talked to her the night before, and Ann wasn't too concerned. But today the phone lines in Ann's area were down, and my mother was panicked. There was no way to contact my brother-in-law during the day, so my mother phoned the Playboy Club. Mom was great on the phone; she had a deceptively pleasant but commanding voice and people went out of their way to accommodate her. After a very long five minutes, the bunny mother came on the line and said Ann had gone home to grab a few things. Her neighborhood was being evacuated.

African Americans, the people we marched for, were on the warpath; they were loud, angry, and violent. The summer sky was dark from the fires. And the sun was blood red, just as it had been the day JFK was shot. Late that first afternoon, Ann managed to phone. She and her daughter were safe at a hotel in downtown Hollywood, and she'd managed to make contact with her husband.

Something was very wrong. Middle-class white citizens were dangerous; we'd seen JFK lose his life to an average joe on a sunny day in Texas. The military was dangerous; we ate dinner in front of the TV watching guys Willy's age dying in Vietnam. Sex was dangerous; I'd seen what Rita went through after her abortion and

during her bout with gonorrhea. Now our neighbors were dangerous; they'd set Los Angeles on fire.

After all that had happened that summer, the Beatle concert at
Dodger Stadium was anti-climactic. Along with Carol and Debbie,
Jeanne brought her uncle's friend's daughter, who had bleached
blond hair and was wearing blue jeans. I felt stupid in my mini
skirt and tights. If I wanted to keep up with the music scene, jeans
were going to be my new uniform.

Chapter Ten

"I'm Up on the Tightrope"
Leon Russell

My mother hated jeans. She believed denim was only appropriate for farmers. But I shrunk my new pair to fit and tried them on in front of the hall mirror. I liked what I saw and retired my bell-bottoms. Mom reminded me I still had to follow school code and wear dresses during the day. She was getting louder and angrier about everything. I was thankful that my brother easily kept himself busy, because I wasn't sure how capable Mom was of caring for him. I also had concern for my grandmother, who was in her eighties and losing her eyesight.

The second day of the fall semester of junior year, I came home to find Nana on the kitchen floor with a bucket, brush, rag, and bar of Fels Naptha soap. Her boney knees were bruised and her face red. I asked what on earth she was doing. "Your mother said the floor needed scrubbing and waxing," she panted. I helped Nana to her feet, took her into the bathroom and cleaned her up, got her into dry clothes, and had her settle into the chair in her bedroom. Then I looked for my mother. Mom didn't drive, but she sure knew how to use the telephone. I found her at the front door, paying a liquor store deliveryman for a bottle of Ten High. She wasn't even trying to hide it anymore.

I asked her why Nana had been on the kitchen floor, which hadn't been particularly dirty in the first place; I swept every day and mopped at least twice a week. Why hadn't Mom scrubbed it herself, if she thought it was so bad? My mother insisted her back hurt and that she just couldn't stand the baseboards anymore. That didn't make sense. I always cleaned the baseboards.

My brother was in the backyard, playing with a piece of pipe my father used in the work he brought home. It had only been a couple of weeks since Paul spent a night projectile vomiting after licking some residue from a similar pipe. I took away the pipe, shut it in the garage, washed Paul's hands, and gave him a toy. Back inside, Mom had called Nana out of the bedroom and was shouting at her. I told Mom she looked tired and said I'd be happy to finish the floor. I had to promise two coats of wax, but that seemed to satisfy her.

I didn't want to burden a girlfriend with my problems at home. Rita's mother slept with sailors not much older than Rita, Yvette's mother tried so hard to be cool she made an ass of herself, Cathi's mom was ill, Katy's mother smacked her around, and Connie's mom just wanted her out of the house. How could I lay my own petty concerns on any of them? So I phoned Joe, just to talk. Sure, everything was fine with me. What was going on with him? He told me he was still waiting for me to turn eighteen. Talking to Joe made me feel better; he always had that effect on me.

The third week of school, during home ec class, I fainted dead away. The nurse called my mother, who phoned for my father to come home from work. I'd been feeling faint for several weeks but hadn't thought much about it. In the car on the way to the doctor, my mother accused me of trying to get out of going to school. *Sure, Mom*, I thought, *I just willed myself to faint.* Then she decided I must be pregnant. I wasn't; my period had just ended, but I knew I was in for a pelvic exam. That could mean big trouble, so I had to think fast.

I had an ally in Mrs. Crane, the doctor's nurse. She locked eyes with me, raised her eyebrows, and smiled. She was thinking. When Dr. Baird said I wasn't "intact," Mrs. Crane reminded him I'd had a pelvic exam a couple of years prior, during a recurring problem with kidney and bladder infections. Even Mom remembered the pain I'd been in after that unnecessary exam. The nurse went on to explain that I had been dancing since I was very small and that constant stretching usually pulled everything aside. I added that my sister had convinced me to use tampons rather than pads, and I said those first few insertions hurt. Mrs. Crane winked at me. One of those stories must have been true because I hadn't bled that first time with Brian. Mom shut up.

A blood test showed I was seriously anemic and that I had mononucleosis. Mono had been going around. It started with Willy, and then spread to Katy and Cheryl. Half of South High had it. Connie was down with it for most of the summer. So I was taken out of school and given a home teacher, a sweet older woman who tutored district students with temporary ailments. She was scheduled to come to the house twice a week. My mother was enraged. She insisted I'd "gotten what I wanted." Although Dr. Baird told my parents to let me socialize when I felt like it, my mother ended all visits from friends, allowing me one brief phone call per evening.

There was no sneaking out of our house. My sister had tried it a couple of times, and when my mother caught her, Ann and I were forced to swap rooms with my parents. That meant my room was at the very back of the house. A door opened onto the backyard, but there was a locking gate on either side. The only other way off the property, aside from the conspicuous front and back doors, was a gate at the very back of the yard that opened onto the Palos Verdes horse trail. Cathi, Connie, Katy, and Cheryl stayed in touch by tapping on my side window late at night and holding up signs. I read them with a flashlight and wrote back. The window didn't open, and although the gate could be climbed, it rattled badly and was easily visible from my parents' bedroom window. Mom wasn't sleeping anymore. She was watching me. A bathroom with a door at each end separated my room from the laundry area and my parents' bedroom, and Mom had my father put a second sliding lock on the inside of the bathroom door, which forced me to take the hall all the way around the house to get to the bathroom. There was no logic to any of it. I assumed my mother needed control over something, and I provided a natural victim.

After a month of insisting I felt much better, my aunt persuaded my parents to have my blood tested again. But Mom liked having someone around. I fixed her breakfast and lunch every day, prepared dinner for the whole family, and kept the house clean. She did the laundry. I don't know why she liked to control everyone's dirty clothes, but that was her domain. After a long and intimate talk with the doctor, Mom had him write a note that would keep me home the entire year. The way Mom saw it, I got along well with the home teacher and my grades were fine. The doctor agreed, but his nurse explained to my mother that I needed to be in school for emotional and psychological reasons. Mrs. Crane had a degree in psychology. She was one of the first honestly liberated women I'd met, and this was pre-women's lib. Mrs. Crane had planned to open a private psychology practice before choosing life as an R.N. It was agreed that I'd be allowed to go back to school after the winter holidays, and that I'd be permitted visits with friends in the meantime.

One evening Cathi showed up. I'd been working steadily for Mrs. Stoddard, and Cathi knew I had some money tucked away. She was trying to collect a whopping fifty dollars from everybody she trusted. She was pregnant. And she was almost three months along. There had just been another L.A. abortion bust, so Cathi needed to go to Mexico. She wanted me to go with her. Gail was out of town with her parents, and Cathi didn't trust anybody else. This was an emergency, and I wasn't about to let her down.

I knew there wasn't a chance my mother would let me out of the house for an entire weekend just for the fun of it. Mom disapproved of fun; laughter made her instantly suspicious. I sat down with my aunt and explained that I felt trapped in the house and would like to visit a friend overnight. My blood work showed I had improved, and I just wanted to get away. She understood. So did Nana, who encouraged me to have a sleepover. My aunt and grandmother were behind me, but Mom rarely listened to anyone. She even had my father scared. I crossed my fingers and asked my aunt to talk to my mother on my behalf.

Cathi told her mom that Gail was going to have another slumber party but that my mother didn't want me to go because she didn't know Gail well enough. Mrs. Willard phoned my mother. Mom finally gave me permission to stay with Cathi at Gail's on Friday night. The story also got Cathi out of the house on Friday, but we needed more time.

I called Ann. My sister had never been afraid of my mother, and she came through for me. She told Mom that as long as I was going to be out Friday night, she could really use me to babysit on Saturday night. Mom bought it. Cathi told her mother she was going to babysit with me. Mrs. Willard never checked up on Cathi. We felt terrible about lying to Cathi's mom, although telling her the truth would have been worse.

The one big problem was that we were sixteen-year-old kids from L.A. We were going to have to lie our way into Mexico. While so many people were trying to sneak out, we needed a way in. Cathi had a fake driver's license she'd successfully used several times; it indicated she was nineteen. We didn't have time to have one made for me. But Rita knew someone who could fake up a birth certificate to make me older. If we got stopped at the border, I'd just say I didn't drive.

Cathi picked me up Friday afternoon, and we immediately got on the freeway heading south. The drive would take about three hours, and we needed to arrive before dark. We were walking a tightwire, because border patrol was lighter during the day. At the final rest stop, Cathi pulled a small tube of weed from her purse and handed me a Tampax. I pulled the tampon out of the cardboard housing and slid the tube of weed inside. Tampon housings weren't terribly comfortable to wear, but barring a full-body search, they provided a way to transport drugs. Cathi swore we'd be safe. She was going to need to get high after the abortion, and I understood.

We prayed we'd just be waved through into Mexico, but no, we were stopped. The guard didn't care much about I.D. He was more concerned that we were kids from L.A. So he and another guy completely inspected the car and searched the trunk. They even checked our headlights, which was then a common place to hide drugs. We were clean. But the stop had held us up, and we didn't get to the clinic until after 8:30. Cathi was late for her appointment.

After a forty-five-minute wait, Cathi was directed to a room. She asked if I could go with her, and nobody seemed to care. A nurse checked Cathi and told her to go home; she was too far along. This had been Cathi's fear, and I saw the look of absolute devastation in her eyes. "She can't be more than two and a half months," I stated. "I'm her roommate. I know when she had sex. Cathi's fiancé left for Vietnam the next day." Cathi was sporting the fake engagement ring we passed around for occasions like this, and Cathi managed to flash it at the nurse without being too obvious. The woman said she'd be back with the doctor.

The doctor agreed to perform the surgery as long as Cathi signed the required high-risk paperwork. When he left the room, we both sighed. Cathi's fake I.D. had a phony address on it, so if there were repercussions, nobody would be able to track her. I thought I'd be asked to sit in the crowded waiting room, but a different doctor came in, pulled on gloves, gave Cathi a spinal block, and began to go to work on her. She was trying not to cry, and we hung onto each other. I kissed her forehead, and she asked me to sing "As Tears Go By," which sent both of us into tears. When the embryo was removed, the doctor began ranting in Spanish. We spoke slow high school Spanish and couldn't figure out what he was saying.

Once Cathi was in a room, a charm-free row of cots where moaning girls were left until their spinal blocks wore off, a woman explained to us that Cathi had been four months pregnant. Cathi tried to lift herself up and cried, "That son of a bitch!" I understood. Cathi only had sex with Larry, except during that one horrible Hollywood weekend four months ago when she'd been (what is now referred to as) date-raped by a member of a popular bubblegum band with a hit record on the charts. As she was being injected with antibiotics, Cathi swore she'd get my money back to me posthaste, and get everyone else their money, too. This guy would pay up fast unless he wanted some nasty publicity. Cathi asked to change the name of the responsible male party on her medical records, and the nurse simply whited-out Larry's name and put in the name of the date rapist. We handed over our last forty dollars for a copy.

On Saturday morning, Cathi had a screaming headache and was still having numbness in her legs, but she was going to have to drive across the border because I didn't have an over-eighteen driver's license. It was hard getting into Mexico, but it was more difficult getting back into the U.S. Cathi was suffering, so I kept a hand on the wheel and talked her through the drive. Later, Cathi referred to it as The Hokey Pokey Ride, because I repeated, "right foot accelerate, left foot clutch, right foot brake," until we hit the border check. Cathi told me she was bleeding through her pads and I stuffed my jacket underneath her. The guard wanted to know what was wrong. I told him Cathi had eaten a bad taco and had an awful case of Montezuma's Revenge. That seemed to upset the guard, because he told me to get Cathi to a doctor, and waved us through to freedom. A half-mile into California, Cathi made a nasty swerve into a gas station, and we changed seats. Cathi changed pads again, climbed into the passenger seat, and started crying.

We got into L.A. in the early afternoon and stopped at a gas station. Cathi threw out her jeans and underwear, along with my jacket. She put on clean clothes and stuffed her underwear with three of the oversized pads the clinic had given her. Then we drove by Rita's and caught her just as she was leaving. Rita had been through a second abortion by now, and we explained what had happened. She took Cathi's temperature, looked her over, pressed on her lower abdomen, and then looked at Cathi's prescription bottle. Rita didn't think we needed to see a doctor, but warned Cathi that if anything changed for the worse, she had to do something fast.

The bleeding had slowed by the time we got to Cathi's house. I explained to Mrs. Willard that Cathi's period was bad and she didn't think she could babysit with me. Cathi's father offered to give me a ride, but I told him I wanted to do some shopping and would take the bus. I promised to check on Cathi later and kissed her goodbye.

Across the street from the Willards' was a J.J. Newberry with a phone vestibule. My sister told me everything was fine there; Mom had called and Ann had reassured her. I had another night to myself, so I called Joe's and Bruce answered. He said he'd drive down and pick me up.

Chapter Eleven

"Young Girls Are Coming to the Canyon"
The Mamas and the Papas

That now-familiar car pulled up and I threw my shoulder bag and my overnight bag, a well-worn old drafting satchel given to me by my aunt, in the back seat. Bruce warned me that ever-cautious Joe probably wouldn't let me stay all night in his house, and I let Bruce know I didn't care. I just wanted to be back in the Canyon.

I asked Bruce to just drop me off on one of the corners. He was going to Joe's house on Amor, but was hesitant about leaving me on the street alone. Finally he dropped me off at the corner, where he gave me his jacket and a five-dollar bill. I told him I didn't need it, but he insisted. He promised to check on Cathi for me, and I swore to call him if anything went wrong.

It was Saturday evening in Laurel Canyon. Despite the cold, I was only one of several girls aimlessly walking with shoulder bags and/or overnight paraphernalia. We were all looking for something to fill the void. One girl invited me to a party, but she was frighteningly stoned. I thanked her but turned her down. At about 8:00, a car slowed next to me, and the driver asked, "Don't you know Charley from the Whiskey?" I said I did, and he gave me his name. I recognized it. He worked as a roadie, most recently with the Hollies. Right now he was staying in L.A. He told me to climb in the car. I convinced myself I wasn't hitchhiking because this guy wasn't a complete stranger. We had friends in common. I wasn't scared. I was home.

We went back to his place. I asked to use the shower, and he told me to make myself at home. I shaved my legs, showered, and perfumed. I brushed my hair and teeth and made up my face. Feeling like I'd washed away Mexico, I returned to the living room. We smoked the untouched weed Cathi had me hide the day before, and found a Jerry Lewis movie on TV. When the National Anthem finally played, he woke me up and led me to bed. Sex was sweet. I liked the skin-to-skin contact and the smell of his hair. He woke me at about 8:30 in the morning. I usually got up at 5:00, but it had been a long couple of days. He drove me to my sister's place, and later in the day, she drove me home. My aunt asked if I'd had a good time, and I told her I didn't understand how her cousin Evelyn, a maternity nurse in a local hospital, could stand her job. Es had no idea what I was talking about or what an auspicious remark it would turn out to be.

Cathi had paid me back within the week. She'd shown her medical records from Mexico to Mr. Big Stuff, and he couldn't pay her off fast enough. The whole incident would have gone far beyond statutory rape. Cathi wouldn't have hesitated to make sure she ruined this guy's reputation as an innocent, goofy guitarist in a popular bubblegum band sponsored by a major television network. This time, Cathi's bluntness paid off.

I'd been back to the Garage, and told my father I'd played a friend's amazing twelve-string electric guitar. My father was fascinated by electric guitars. He liked both music and electronics, and the combination amazed him. I knew we didn't have much money, practically everything in the house was homemade, but he asked me if I wanted an electric guitar for Christmas. He could get a cheap amp from a friend at work. At first I didn't believe him, but on Christmas, he came through with a bottom-of-the-line electric guitar. Katy and Cheryl also scored electric guitars; Cheryl's was a bass and she was getting good. We still didn't have a reliable drummer, but our band was starting to come together. During my trips to the Garage, I had typically learned more about rock guitar in one afternoon or evening than Katy and I had managed to figure out on our own over the past two years. The group of us could now crank out some serious rock music. But on Christmas night, my mother drunkenly stumbled and sprained her foot. The bleak reality of my home life set in, and Katy and I spent Christmas night lying on my bed, staring at the ceiling, our new electric guitars discarded against the wall in the dark.

My aunt's colleague, Mr. Brown, had gotten himself a new car for Christmas and wanted to sell his old Nash. It was an ugly little car, white and square, but he'd taken incredible care of it. I spoke up and told him my good friend Cathi had been driving her mother's car and really needed one of her own. Mrs. Willard was ill, and Cathi didn't want to leave her at home without transportation when Mr. Willard was at work. Mr. Brown said that if it was for a friend of mine, he'd let the Nash go for two hundred bucks.

I phoned Cathi and announced that Mr. Brown was selling his old car for two hundred, and I just knew she'd want it. Cathi converted my words from babble to a plea for help, and told me to call her back when I could explain what she should do. When Mom retreated into her bedroom, I phoned Cathi again and hurriedly said that I needed her to buy the car and then transfer the papers to me. Cathi cautioned me about parking on my block. Everyone on the block was on a first name basis (neighbors were friends in the fifties and sixties) and my mother would hear about me and the car within minutes. I phoned Ann, whose old high school chum lived about a half mile away toward the bottom of the hill. If Lynn would let me park on her street, I'd just have to hike down the hill and I'd be free.

I needed a fast two hundred bucks. Connie bought my gorgeous suede boots. Rita paid me to commit a minor crime that caused me to take a frightening look at my scruples, and my need for freedom won out. I asked Mrs. Stoddard for a fifty-dollar loan against work. My sister hired Katy and me to paint her living room and paid us in advance so I could get the money to Mr. Brown. I was close, and Cathi loaned me the last forty bucks. After all, she said, fair was fair.

I was thrilled to be getting my own transportation, but that excitement was tempered by the news that after thirteen years, Mom was "excused" from teaching Sunday school and my parents were quitting church. I was surprised Mom had managed to maintain a sober Sunday morning image as long as she had. Apparently her pride made an exit along with that hour-a-week volunteer job, because she had my father get rid of their double bed and bought twin beds. She stopped caring for her appearance, which surprised everyone. Mom had been a vain and beautiful woman, a dancer and a model, but now wore tacky housecoats and sensible shoes. She cut her enviable long black hair and let it go gray. And she started keeping her bottle of Ten High under the sink in the bathroom, where she could conveniently take a slug out of a Dixie cup.

My father knew something was very wrong, and took me into the garage one day. He confessed that if he weren't afraid for Paul, he'd divorce Mom. He never knew what she might do. None of us did. My aunt and grandmother holed up in their part of the house, in the original bedrooms and small bath that existed before the re-model job several years earlier. Nana and my aunt ate at the kitchen table; my mother didn't want them at the living room table with us. After all, we lived on top of "the hill," which had started out as a field with a few low-income houses but was rapidly becoming a crowded upper-middle-class neighborhood.

There we were, with my aunt and my father working long hours, and my widowed grandmother with her Social Security, trying hard to keep us afloat and present a reasonable image. My brother still wasn't old enough for kindergarten but would soon mistakenly be assessed as emotionally handicapped because of my mother's dismal parenting skills. I was held accountable for every move I made and underwent regular room, purse, and pocket checks. Home was no longer where my heart was. I wanted to be in the Canyon.

One quiet afternoon, my mother hissed at me to come into her bedroom. She locked the door and instructed me to sit down. She needed to talk to someone, and apparently I was the "only one" she could trust. I asked her if she'd rather talk to a friend, or to my aunt, or even my sister. She whispered that she couldn't trust anybody anymore. My grandmother "watched all the time." Mom could see her shadow. My aunt "always got everything her way." My sister had "deserted her." So I sat and listened, continuously gulping in an attempt to send my heart back down to my chest where it belonged. Mom said she'd been having a terrible pain in her right side, and that she was retaining a lot of water. Her stomach had become disproportionately large over the past couple of years; the bulge was embarrassingly mistaken by others for pregnancy several times. But it wasn't water retention, and we all knew it. Then Mom whispered that she'd been vomiting up blood every couple of days. Did I think it was anything serious? Should she be concerned? I told her to ask old Dr. Baird, not me. I was sixteen and the most serious thing I'd seen was my grandfather die after a stroke, and this situation was completely different. I wanted to say, "Mom, you're drinking yourself to death and you know it," but I simply repeated my suggestion that she visit the doctor. Mom swore me to secrecy. I must have sworn to keep quiet, "no matter what," a dozen times before she let me leave her room that day. I kept her secret through her upcoming near-fatal medical complications and then on beyond her death. Until now.

When I was stuck at home, I watched *Where the Action Is*, wrote music, and tried to keep peace between my parents and my grandmother and aunt.

There was nothing comforting about home. But I was finally heading back to school, and now I had a driver's license in my boot, and my own car parked in front of Lynn's house.

Chapter Twelve

"Angel of the Morning"
Juice Newton

I'd started crying and couldn't seem to control it. And when I cried, even softly, my mother got angry. One evening the Turtles had a gig near Vickie's house, and Vickie wanted Jeanne and me to go to the show with her. Jeanne bowed out, but I went to the Cosgroves' and was ushered into Vickie's bedroom. As she finished dressing, I burst into tears. Vickie did her best to calm me down, but I couldn't stop crying. Vickie's mother wanted to know what was wrong, and Vickie said she thought I was upset about my mother's drinking. Vickie's mother said, "Margaret?! She wouldn't drink! She's a lovely person!" And Mrs. Cosgrove drove me home in stony silence. It amazed me that Mom still had people fooled. She drank from morning until night, and didn't know what she was doing half the time. Everyone in the family was terrified of upsetting her. Yet even in a cheap housecoat, Mom could put on a facade that would fool the queen. My doctor's nurse, Mrs. Crane, knew. I think Jeanne's parents knew. My friends knew because they saw it. But for the most part, Mom fooled the world.

I have no idea if the family dynamics were what caused all the crying. I just knew I couldn't control it. It was hard to be cheerful around my friends. I drifted through school days doing just enough work to get satisfactory grades, spent Saturdays in Cheryl's garage with Katy, Cheryl, and Donna (our temporary drummer, borrowed from another all-girl band), and every night I could, hiked down the hill to my car and headed for the Canyon.

Mrs. Willard's health was declining rapidly, and Cathi's father started drinking. Fortunately Cathi had a cousin, Elise, who often spent weekends at the house and, newly married but not working, was free to help out. I guiltily used Mrs. Willard's illness as an excuse to spend nights away from home. My mother knew Cathi depended on me. When Cathi had her wisdom teeth pulled, she wanted me to stay with her. When Cathi had her purse stolen, Cathi ran to me. When Cathi got in a wreck on Robertson Boulevard, I was the first person she called. So when I told my mother that Mrs. Willard was having a bad day, I usually got permission to spend the night with the family. And I was pretty sure Cathi would, as she promised, cover for me.

I wasn't one of those groupies who kept names, dates, and ratings of sexual performance. I didn't collect souvenirs, like Cynthia Plaster Caster. I wasn't chasing anyone in particular. And sex wasn't the main objective; any of us girls could have had sex every night if we'd wanted. I stopped coloring my hair dark and ironing it; I didn't want to be mistaken for Cher anymore. My hair was hip length and auburn, and fell in Renaissance curls. My uniform was jeans and a white lace crop top that exposed my middle. I was one of the Canyon girls. We cared so much we couldn't stand to feel it. We were a sad bunch.

Late one Friday afternoon, I was walking past the Hullabaloo Club. John Sebastian pulled up and motioned me over to the car; he was on the passenger side and I couldn't see who was driving. He said, "Great hair," reached for the back of my neck, and pulled me in to kiss him. We necked for two or three minutes with somebody behind him leaning on their horn. As he and his buddy drove away, John smiled and shouted, "Thanks!" I'd spent a couple of minutes kissing the mouth that sang "Daydream" and "Jug Band Music." Little incidents like that kept me going.

They had to be musicians. I'd do anything for a musician. They created the music that made me feel good. It was possibly the only thing that made any of us feel good.

On a foggy Friday, I gave my name to a new guy at the back door of the Troubadour, and he waved me backstage. The Byrds were booked that night, and were sitting around smoking weed. Michael, who'd slept with Yvette a year or two earlier, motioned me over. I thought he'd kiss me, which was a common rock star/ groupie greeting, but he sat me down next to him, asked someone for a pen, and handed me the address of a house in the hills. When the group was finished for the night, Michael nodded in a 007 way, so I got in the Nash and made my way through the fog. There were two girls in the living room and a couple of guys in the kitchen. Michael took me right into the bedroom. I stayed until a stab of morning sunlight woke me. Michael was out cold, his face buried in my hair, so I eased my way out of bed, kissed him on the forehead, and walked out. Some guy waved goodbye to me as I left the house.

Joe found out I'd become a Canyon girl. As before, he sat me down and asked if I was sure I knew what I was doing. I wanted to say, "Well damn, you were my first choice," but told him I was fine and not to worry. A year earlier I would have done anything for Joe, but now he was another person to answer to.

I'd seen Katy at school, but we hadn't gotten together for a while. She caught up with me at lunch one day. She'd run into Ian Whitcomb at Capitol Records. He was in town with his brother, Robin, who had been keeping scrapbooks of Ian's musical success. There was a photo of Jeanne, Katy, and me included in one of the binders. Robin had shown the photo to Cher, and she'd commented on my resemblance to her. Katy arranged for us to meet Robin for lunch.

Robin was young, cute, funny, and an absolute gentleman. He bought us lunch and asked about school. He knew we were kids, and he didn't care; he seemed to enjoy the light conversation. When we left the café, Robin asked if we'd like to meet Sonny and Cher. Their house was his next stop. We'd seen them plenty of times on stage, and agreed to go along for the ride.

The public Sonny and Cher presented the quintessential flower child couple image, despite the fact that everyone knew Sonny was considerably older than we flower children and was vocally anti-drugs. Members of the network swore Sonny and Cher weren't even married, as they publicly claimed. (Living together was still deliciously scandalous.) We remembered the couple as the nerdy Caesar and Cleo, but since then we thought they'd become kind of cool. Their estate told us something different. The two expensive cars inside the gated driveway weren't cool cars; they were old-money, conservative collectibles. Nothing about the house said flower child. It said, "We're conservative; we have money, and we want to show it off." I felt slightly betrayed.

Cher was nice but not at all what I expected. She was wearing designer slacks and what appeared to be a cashmere sweater; her now-famous hair was pulled back into a clip. She looked like a wealthy housewife. The fact that she was barefoot, though, made her seem more acceptable. She had a warm smile and greeted us with hugs. Sonny was at the other end of the room, either busy or attempting to appear busy. He greeted us in suit slacks, a white shirt, and slip-on shoes. If his hair had been shorter, he would have looked like the flower child movement's nemesis, the establishment. Cher remarked that she and I really did look alike, and asked Katy and me where we lived, if we were still in school, and otherwise created pleasant chatter. She asked me what kind of foundation I wore on my face (none) and what kind of cologne I was wearing (Shalimar). We were beginning to feel more comfortable, so Katy mentioned that we spent a lot of time in the Canyon.

Hearing this, Sonny strutted into the middle of the room and demanded, "Do you really think that your behavior is smart? Do you feel safe? What do your parents think?" and so forth. I'd never run across such arrogance before.

Katy popped off with, "Sonny, everybody wants to know when you and Cher got married." Sonny shot her a look that shut her up. Cher was unfortunately caught in the middle of this. Robin knew that Katy and I felt insulted and made excuses for us to leave. I continued to admire Cher's singing ability, but from then on I could only give Sonny credit for business acumen.

I came home from school the following Friday to find my grandmother in tears and my brother asleep on her bed. Nana had been babysitting again, which meant my mother had probably passed out. Mom had accused Nana of not paying her fair share. That didn't compute. My parents decided to move to California in the forties and convinced my grandparents and aunt to come along so my mother could afford to buy the California house she'd always wanted. My father was a hardworking blue-collar high school dropout, but my grandfather had been an art professor with specialized graining skills. My aunt was an art designer for *Vogue* who later became a draftsperson. It had always been obvious to me that Mom was using her parents and her sister to get what she wanted, and I knew that Nana and my aunt paid plenty to keep that household running. Was this a serious accusation or had Mom simply run out of cash for her daily delivery of Ten High and attacked Nana in a panic? I'd seen her pay the delivery guy with quarters more than once. I turned on my grandmother's TV, fixed her a sandwich, and explained that I was going to spend the night with Cathi and her family. Then I told my mother to have another drink and walked out. I didn't know what the repercussions to my remark might be, and at the moment I didn't care.

It was late afternoon when Charley, my old Sunset Strip buddy, called to me from the door of the Whiskey. He thought Donovan was inside but wasn't sure. He pointed to a figure sitting at the back in the dark, apparently drinking white wine. Charley was full of questions. Did that sound like Donovan? Wasn't Donovan into serious drugs? Was Donovan in town for some reason? Shadow, a dead ringer for Bob Dylan and a denizen of the Strip, joined the conversation. "It's weird, "Shadow whispered, "he doesn't even talk." I loved Donovan's music. I worshipped him. If he was inside, I was going to meet him. I called Tina Van Voorhees to see if Donovan had been through the airport, but nobody answered at her place. I managed to catch Rita, who swore she'd get in touch with her uncle and call me back at the Whiskey. Then it struck me. "Why do you think it isn't Donovan?" I asked. Charley explained that when the guy walked through the back door, one of the girls said, "Hi Donovan," and Donovan said, "Ah, but am I really who you think I am? I could be an illusion, you could be an illusion, this could all be an illusion." This struck me as unbearably naive on Charley's part. The comment sounded like a wisecrack, or if the guy was stoned, possibly a drug-induced revelation. Charley and Shadow decided I would be the one to verify the identity of the guy at the back of the room. I cursed them both.

There were two girls inside, getting things ready for the night's crowd. I accepted a Coke from Charley and walked toward the back of the room. I saw a youngish, long-haired guy pouring wine from a bottle into a paper cup. I would never have doubted it was Donovan, but as Shadow pointed out, we could be a room full of fakes. Shadow was constantly being asked for his autograph by those mistaking him for Bob Dylan, and I'd spent a lot of time cashing in on my resemblance to Cher.

I smiled at the guy and he smiled back. If this wasn't Donovan, he had to be a clone. I felt a rush of excitement. He held up the bottle and raised his eyebrows. I said thanks but that I didn't drink, then sat down several feet away and dropped my purse on the floor. Charley and Shadow were gesturing to me. They looked like a bad mime act that would have been booed off even an amateur stage. I knew what they wanted but refused to be the uncool one to giggle, "Ooooh, are you really Donovan?"

After about ten minutes of feeling like a jerk, I heard, "Hey, sweetheart." He'd spoken. British, with a bit of a brogue. I knew Donovan had been born in Scotland, but I typically couldn't tell one accent from another. And I knew how well people could fake accents; Willy successfully did it all the time. Charley and Shadow really did have me questioning my own eyes and ears. I turned. "Are you staying for the show?" he asked. I told him I hadn't planned to and asked if he was performing. He shook his head. Another ten minutes passed in silence. Then he spoke again. "You play guitar," he stated. He'd noticed I had short nails on my left hand and longer ones on my right. Suddenly he stood up, took my hands, and said, "Good for you, sweetheart, you use steel strings." I told him they simply sounded better, that nylon strings seemed cheap. He agreed. Then he told me I sang. I had to dispute that. I could carry a tune and I could harmonize, but I sure couldn't sing like Katy. Finally he walked out into the light, and Charley and Shadow visibly backed away. "Do you have an acoustic?" he asked.

Charley produced an acoustic guitar from the side of the stage and handed it over like he was feeding a cobra. I leaned in towards Charley and said, "It's him, you dummy." The guitar was then passed along to me. "Sing something," he smiled. I panicked. I was, without a doubt, going to make an absolute ass of myself. Donovan was a god to me. But I tuned the guitar and did "The Cruel War." He smiled and nodded and asked for another song. I wasn't about to play a Donovan song; that would be just too embarrassing. So I did Dylan's "Don't Think Twice, It's All Right." I'd learned an intricate pick that was perfect for the song, and he noticed. "Nice job; I admire the pick." I offered him the guitar, but he shook his head. Another couple of minutes passed in silence before he asked if I wanted to grab something to eat. I said sure, and he picked up my shoulder bag, slung it over his own shoulder, and we walked out. I looked back to see Charley gesturing like mad. I smiled.

We picked at deli food. My still-unverified pal didn't say much, but he smiled almost constantly. When we'd both stopped playing with our food, he asked if I'd like to stop by his hotel. I nodded almost too anxiously, and as we walked, we received a lot of stares. I was hoping someone would ask for an auto-graph, but no one did. We ended up at one of the small Span-ish-style hotels. It was largely hidden by trees and not at all the type of place most of the big stars stayed. I expected someone to call my buddy by name but no one did. They just nodded respectfully.

His suite was smallish but elegant. It had an organic, almost fantasy-like feel that suited him. Suitcases were stacked in the main room. There were two guitar cases against the wall, both acoustics, and a guitar propped on the sofa. I nodded at the guitar and said, "Fair's fair, play me a song." He perched on the arm of the sofa and sang "Catch the Wind." I knew that song inside and out, and I loved that man.

He offered me a drink, and I requested my standard tonic and lemon. Then it struck me that my car was parked in a bad spot and I asked to use the phone. I told Charley where to find my spare key, and he assured me that he'd move the car to a safe place. He asked me if I'd seen any Donovan identification. I told Charley to knock it off because ultimately it didn't matter one way or another; I liked this guy. I had been politely left alone during my phone call, so I took the opportunity to ask why Charley was so fascinated with this particular star. Charley worked with big names every day; he'd met enormously famous musicians. "That guy just struck me as odd," Charley said. I trusted Charley, and suddenly felt uneasy. I was put on hold briefly, then Charley came back on the line to say Rita had phoned. Donovan was in town, recording at CBS. I started to say, "No joke?" when Charley laughed and hung up on me. His laughter broke my tension and I relaxed.

The hotel room was cool and dark, and for a long wonderful time we played folk music and shared guitar picking methods. Once this remarkable man loosened up, he laughed a lot. I knew he wasn't very much older than me, and I felt like I was with an-other kid. It was both exciting and comfortable.

At about nine o'clock, he put down his guitar, broke open an-other bottle of wine, poured just half a glass for himself, and sat down next to me. "Now," he said, "what goes on behind that enchanting face?" I told him he didn't need to know; most guys didn't want to hear a girl chatter on about herself. He studied me and said, "You're lonely." That made me tear up, and he leaned in and kissed me. "And you're different," he added. "There's something going on about you." He stood and held out his hand, which was the standard "we're going to bed now" gesture.

I expected sex with him to be romantic and gentle. But it was the wildest sex I'd had yet, incredibly funny and silly. Within ten minutes, we'd pulled the bedding onto the floor with us and had managed to knot the sheets. At about midnight, when I decided it was an appropriate time to leave, he anxiously convinced me to stay. We pulled the bedding back on the bed, and went at it again before falling asleep. When sunlight first filtered through the blinds in the morning, he propped himself on one elbow, kissed me just once, and said, "I could love a girl like you." Sure it was a line. I didn't care. We had messy, tangled sex a last time and he tickled me until I was in tears.

I brushed my teeth and hair, and put on my clothes. He walked me all the way back to the Whiskey. Nobody was around yet. I found the Nash, waiting patiently. My latest love wrapped his fingers in my hair and asked me to give him my phone number. I couldn't. He wasn't just a real rock star. He was a folk singer. Somebody whose music made me feel everything from giddy to morose. He was God. Ironically, the last thing he said as I drove away was, "I don't even have your name."

When I passed the Whiskey later that week, Charley confronted me on the sidewalk. He asked why I hadn't checked luggage tags. I admitted that suitcases had been in plain sight the whole night, but it just never occurred to me to sneak a look. I said I felt stupid, and Charley told me to go with the feeling. Charley, his curiosity still unsatisfied, piled me in his car and asked for directions to the hotel where I'd spent that remarkable night. At the front desk, we asked if Donovan Leitch was in his room. The clerk told us he'd checked out.

A lot of the people on the Strip joined local college students to protest the war. I was concerned but hadn't gotten out there and spoken up yet. Then one day Cathi phoned and told me that Roger, an older classmate who'd graduated last June, had been killed in Nam. Pictures of Roger scrolled through my mind. I could hear Roger deliberately trying to make me blush by cracking dirty jokes in math class. I could see Roger standing on the jock circle, playing guitar and singing "Satisfaction" entirely off-key. I could feel Roger's strong arm around me on the way to the nurse's office when I fell and got a rock lodged in my left knee.

I joined the protests, writing dozens of letters and talking to anyone who would listen. I got a fatigue shirt, stitched an upside-down American flag on the back, and embroidered "Roger" underneath. Far too many other names were added to that shirt over the next few years. We chanted and sang at protests, and in a couple of years, we'd be singing Donovan's "Universal Soldier."

Chapter Thirteen

"There's Something Happening Here"
Buffalo Springfield

I turned seventeen in spring. Just one more year at home and I could leave for good. Parents still held absolute domain over children. To fight with or defy one's parents typically ended in a kid being sent up ("sent up the river") to juvenile detention. I knew a couple of guys who spent time in detention, and once out they were never the same. Girls who misbehaved were typically shipped off to stay with a strict relative such as a formidable aunt who believed in physical punishment. I had a couple of those in Virginia, so I planned to be careful for the next twelve months.

The Strip wasn't as alive as it had been earlier in the year. Curfew laws were so strict that kids were being taken to jail for simply walking from clubs to their cars. We were scared because, with the exception of Willy, we were all still underage. None of our parents knew we got into eighteen-and-over clubs. If they found out, we'd be grounded for life.

Canyon girls were being hassled for walking the public canyon roads, sometimes even during the day. Club managers were harassed and there were almost nightly underage-drinking bust attempts in clubs all along the Strip. Katy was taken to jail three times in one month for driving with a legitimate license; the cops thought she looked too young to drive. Each time Katy's parents verified her age via telephone, those damned cops still managed to hold her another couple of hours. It wasn't just young girls, or only club or shop owners, it was anybody who appeared to be under the age of thirty. The cops had cracked down on the entire counterculture. We hated them.

I felt safe at Joe's, at the Garage, and typically inside the Whiskey or the Troubadour where I knew the management would give a high sign to split if necessary. But I didn't roam around much and never strayed far from the car.

My mother couldn't decide whether I was her best friend or her worst enemy. She'd call me into her room to talk, thank me for keeping her secret, and tell me I was the only one she could trust. Then she'd turn around and say I didn't know all of her secrets and demand to know just who I thought I was. Her face was puffy and her hands swollen. For the first time in her life, she began to put on weight, bouncing up from 105 pounds to 130 in just a couple of months. My grandmother, frail with dimming eyesight, was still being ordered around. My aunt did her best to keep the peace, but she was fighting a losing battle. My father simply retreated to the garage when he was home. I was just waiting for something to happen.

Because it was frightening at home and dangerous on the streets of Hollywood, I began hanging out at Joe's gigs. I typically paid my way in. Joe rarely knew I was there. When we did talk, it felt safe and good. The more time I spent with him, the more I learned about the guy behind that incredible facade, and the more I understood what had attracted me to him in the first place.

I found a note on my bed one afternoon. Vickie had phoned. It'd been a long time, so I called her right away. She'd met a new band called Ordinary Men, and had shown her picture collection to some of the guys. Steve, lead singer and lead guitar, wanted to meet me. Did I want to go to a concert?

I'd heard Ordinary Men on the radio and always managed to confuse them with the Troggs. They could rock it like "Wild Thing" or mellow it out like "Love Is All Around," but it was always sensual. I thought they might make it if they could put their own unique twist on their music. Vickie asked if I'd seen the guys. I hadn't, and with the latest downtown problems, I wasn't taking any chances just because some guy liked my picture. If the situation wasn't safe, I wasn't going. The one thing I wouldn't risk was trouble with the ruthless and uncompassionate gang of cowboys Los Angeles called "cops."

Vickie checked the schedule for Ordinary Men and got back to me. They were playing a charity event in Santa Monica on a Saturday afternoon. What could be safer than that?

She picked me up in her own seventeenth-birthday present, a terrific bright yellow car, bought brand new by her father. We arrived at the auditorium midday, found a nearby restaurant, and talked over a long lunch. Her life was so different from mine. She was hanging out with Tony Dow of *Leave It To Beaver* fame, and spent her time surfing, playing volleyball, and going to formal dances. She was living a traditional teenage lifestyle and seemed happy.

At the show, we yawned our way through a couple of amateur opening acts. The place was full of very young girls. Vickie commented how we'd looked like that just two or three years prior, and I had to agree. There was a break between the openers and Ordinary Men, and I noticed a couple of people on stage arguing about a piece of equipment. One of the guys caught my attention. He was wiry, with tons of wavy hair falling around his face. His eyes were huge, and he had Mick Jagger's mouth. Vickie pointed to him. "That's Steve," she said.

The music started out great. When song number three ended, an older man signed for a time-out, and when Ordinary Men came back on they sounded almost tranquilized, singing old Beatle music and a few bubblegum songs. When the first set was over, the guys signed autographs. Vickie took me backstage just as Steve stormed into the room shouting that the management knew his music and if they didn't like it, they could stick their charity up their asses. Although Ordinary Men was performing free, they had been asked to dumb it down for the mid-afternoon all-ages audience. Steve pulled out a cigarette, glanced over at Vickie and me, and said, "You brought her." He greeted me as "Guinevere" and offered me a cigarette. His bassist offered a Coke, which I took instead. Steve seemed comfortable in his own skin and I liked that. We talked for a few minutes, and then he was back on stage.

Vickie's mother knew Steve's mother, who had been searching for Steve for the past year. He'd gone to a local high school and graduated at sixteen. Steve was only seventeen, my age. But he had his own place in Hermosa Beach and a fake I.D that indicated he was twenty-two and had a completely different last name. Vickie explained that Steve's parents, wealthy alcoholics, had sent him to juvenile detention once too often, and he'd decided to leave home. They didn't even know about the band. Steve had a gorgeous face and would have looked great in a ponytail, but he kept his hair framing his face to be less recognizable when on television. He moved about once a month. Right now he was at a live-in hotel, in one of those suites with a kitchen area and separate bedroom. Steve's parents hated rock music; the juvenile detention time had been for "giving his mother a nervous breakdown" with his music and then refusing to stay silent. He was considered "out of hand." Rock was Steve's passion, so after his mom turned him in the second time, he decided to leave for good. I understood.

I didn't fall into bed with Steve. I really didn't want to get mixed up in his life. I needed to keep myself safe until I was eighteen, and Steve was potential trouble. He was teenage trouble. The worst kind.

Although I didn't sleep with Steve (I'd grown accustomed to one-nighters with older guys) I liked his company. One day we went up into the canyons to visit an old school friend of Steve's, and got lost. We pulled over onto the dirt by the side of the road and got out of Steve's secondhand VW bug.

Steve was wild. He scooted out onto the side of the canyon, gave himself a shove, and successfully slid halfway to the bottom before turning head over heels a couple of times. "I'm alive!" he grinned, and then encouraged me to join him. People had died falling down those canyons. So I climbed down the coward's way, and had to laugh out loud when I saw Steve close up. He was filthy. He'd gone head first into the dirt. His embroidered shirt was torn. He struck me as incredibly nuts, and amazingly attractive.

We had crazy, dirty sex in one of the canyons under the midday sun. A couple of guys must have spotted us, because we heard a wolf whistle and a "You go for it!" from far above. Afterward, we climbed back up to Steve's car, shook the dirt out of our hair and clothes, and got into the car laughing. I couldn't get comfortable. Back at his place, I found leaves lodged in my underwear.

I started seeing Steve a couple times a week. When he did feel the need to change residences, he made sure he stayed close. He'd lived off the Strip earlier in the year, but with the latest rash of busts, was now sticking to the beach.

Everybody wanted to be part of the curfew protest. The one exception was Steve, who knew better than to risk getting in trouble with the cops. We sat on Cathi's friend's front lawn in West L.A. and painted signs. We were ready, even though Charley warned me to stay away. Steve, Connie, Connie's latest boyfriend, Cathi, and I drove into Hollywood, but the streets were already blocked off. Connie took the back way toward Sunset, and straight into a foul-smelling mist. This meant big trouble. We looped around through the neighborhood and Cathi told us to slow down at an old brown house. An African American buddy we knew from the Flying Jib lived there. As we turned into his driveway he ran out, jumped in the back seat, and shouted, "Split!" We raced out of there.

Our favorite radio stations were playing very little music; instead, local disc jockeys were telling everyone to stay away from the Strip. Things had gotten out of control. All of us had friends who worked down there, and we were concerned. Once out of the area, we found a double pay phone and started calling the clubs. We got very few answers. At Cathi's house, we turned on the evening news. It was worse than any of us could have imagined. Two days later, we learned that Katy suffered two cracked ribs from a billy club. That was just wrong.

It took months for Hollywood to return to anything resembling normal. We had never trusted the cops; now we hated them with a vengeance.

SECTION THREE
The Last Gasps of the Sixties

Chapter Fourteen

"Kind of a Drag"
The Buckinghams

On the first day of senior year, I rushed out the front door, down the porch steps, and fell flat on my face. Jeanne's dad was driving us to school, and he waited patiently while I doctored my knees, changed my torn nylons, and quickly inserted a tampon. The minor accident finally started my overdue period.

That first Friday, Katy, Connie, Cheryl, Cathi, and I went into Hollywood. Each of our mothers thought we were spending the night with a girlfriend, which was, in essence, true. Rita was with Ed again, and Gail was getting serious about a guy who planned to move to Canada to avoid the draft. That left just the five of us. We visited our favorite spots, and then got our own hotel room. It was a high school slumber party, although most of us really couldn't be classified as girls anymore. We talked about the upcoming release of the pill, compared the sexual abilities of musicians we'd slept with, sang racy new lyrics to our favorite songs, and ordered desserts from room service. Some great weed Connie scored gave us a nice, gentle buzz. And we made a pact that if any of us survived to see the age of fifty, we'd all commit suicide. It was a blood oath.

Later in the evening, Cathi removed a tampon housing from between her legs and displayed some hash. We got wasted. Connie asked if smoking dope that had been pulled out of somebody's crotch made us gay, which for one of those stoned-only reasons struck us all extremely funny. Katy eventually got around to those first sexual experiences, and then turned to me and said, "You never did tell us who first screwed you." I must have looked upset, because Connie immediately said, "It's none of our business, Kate." Cathi popped off again with, "Oh, she probably doesn't even know his name; I told you she met some guy in the Canyon." And I shouted, "Brian Jones, you dimwit! I got nailed by Brian Jones! Okay?!" After an initial look of mild surprise all around, Katy said, "Well damn, Cathi, she knows his name," and everybody laughed hysterically. That night was the last time we were all just girls together.

The following week, Cathi and I visited Joe. He'd heard about Steve and wanted to make sure I really loved the guy before I got in too deep. I stood looking up at Joe, and felt like a liar when I told him Steve was the one. Joe brought out the truth in me, even when I refused to verbalize it.

Two weeks later, Joe and a couple of his buddies came down to the beach. It was a warm, dark night, and Joe pressed up against me when he hugged me, running both hands down my back and over my hips. He didn't let go. I half-jokingly asked, "When's it going to be time?" Joe said we'd waited long enough. He wanted me to visit him in Laurel Canyon. I didn't know if he was kidding, if he'd gotten confused and thought I'd turned eighteen, or if he'd just given in. But either fear or fate intervened, because every time I planned to drive to Joe's, something happened to stop me.

Toward the end of fall I began feeling sick and dizzy. I couldn't have mono again, not senior year. I was so close to being eighteen and able to escape my mother. I didn't say anything. I was determined to make it to school every day, no matter what.

My aunt was leaving for the supermarket one Saturday and approached me, list in hand. She asked if I needed anything. I thanked her but shook my head. "Don't you need Tampax by now?" she asked. I checked the bathroom cabinet and still had a full box. "I'm stocked," I told her.

I thought back. I'd started my last period the first day of school, which had been three months ago. And it had been a weird period; it only lasted a day. I was late. Really late. And I'd been dizzy and sick. I phoned Cathi.

"Do something now!" she hissed, "I'll go with you." I agreed, and phoned Rita, Tina Van Voorhees, and Cathy Costa. They all got back to me later in the day, and agreed that due to two L.A. abortion busts and problems in Tijuana, Juarez was the place to go. I knew that even with my sister's help I wouldn't be able to stay away long enough to fly to Juarez and back. So Cathi came over, and once my mother fell asleep, we got back on the phone. Cathy Costa made calls of her own and found one doctor in private practice in Tijuana who had just worked on a friend of a friend. It was an overnight deal and seemed to be my only bet. Cathy promised to call back within half an hour.

The phone rang twenty-some minutes later, and I gestured to Cathi to pick it up. I was out back smoking the first cigarette I'd had since early freshman year and came back into the room to hear Cathi tell Steve, "Because you knocked her up, asshole." Steve demanded to talk to me, and Cathi handed over the phone. I told him I wasn't sure what was going on. Maybe I was just sick. He wanted to come over, but I told him I'd talk to him later.

Underage girls were required to have parental accompaniment in order to have a pregnancy test, and even on the rare occasions that happened, we didn't get results for a week. I phoned my sister, who contacted her doctor. He agreed to give me a test if Ann brought me in. I told Steve not to panic, and the first of the week Cathi and I went with Ann to her doctor.

After a pelvic exam and rabbit test, I learned I was four months pregnant. When I got the word, I called Cathi. "Four months?!" she shouted, "and you didn't know?" I reminded her that she'd been four months along when we went to Tijuana for her abortion.

Cathy Costa's contact didn't know if the doctor in Mexico would do the job, but I didn't have another choice. I made an appointment for the following weekend.

Two nights later, Steve showed up. I'd been steering clear of him. I felt so incredibly stupid. For some reason, I'd felt safe with him. He was the one guy I knew willing to use condoms, and I kept actual douche equipment at his place. Steve wanted to get married. After all, my parents thought he was a twenty-two year old musician who was interested in my music. Maybe they'd okay a marriage. I reminded Steve he wasn't twenty-two, as his driver's license indicated. He was seventeen. And if we tried to get married, the truth would come out. Steve would be back in juvenile detention, and I'd be living with a sadistic aunt in Virginia.

Steve, Cathi, and I managed to get into Mexico on time, during the day. But as soon as the doctor began a pelvic exam, he stopped and said, "No." In excellent English he reaffirmed I was at least four months pregnant. There was no convincing him to perform an abortion, and he wouldn't recommend anyone else. It was a long drive home.

My mother noticed I'd stopped wearing jeans. Since the trip to Mexico, I'd been forced to wear mini dresses. The nausea had subsided, but I continued to stumble from dizzy spells. Despite her Ten High high, Mom put two and two together and took me to old Dr. Baird. Now that she knew I was pregnant, hell opened up.

Mom sobbed loudly and constantly, asking me how I could have done this to her. Her friends, those people she still had fooled, only knew she was in some kind of crisis and came to console her. Oh, poor Margaret! How was she going to get through this "nervous breakdown?" Poor Margaret had a long and confidential conversation with the doctor and came back with the news that I'd been pulled out of school, I was going to give up the baby, and my visiting and phone rights were gone. Locks were put on the outsides of the doors to my room with the exception of the hall door. That door was visible from the living room, and heaven forbid a visitor might notice a lock where one didn't belong. Mom had my father put a padlock on the inside of that particular door and, as far as I knew, he threw away the key. The central house heater was in the living room next to the hall door, so when that door was closed for the last time, my room became extremely cold. I was very literally a prisoner. A cold one.

My mother allowed me minimal monthly checkups. She was so terrified of the embarrassment my pregnancy might cause her that she had my father pull the car up into the backyard. I then climbed in the back seat and scrunched down so I wouldn't be seen. I didn't know anything about being pregnant; none of us girls did. I didn't understand the physiology, and I was utterly clueless about the legalities. I didn't know my rights; I wasn't sure if I had any. I'd never heard the term "unfit mother" before. But during my first checkup, the doctor and my mother told me that if I even thought about keeping the baby, they'd have me declared unfit and the child would be taken away.

Mom and Dr. Baird arranged an anonymous county adoption. I wouldn't even see the baby. I'd sign it away ahead of time and it would be taken from me in the delivery room. I was assigned a social worker, a middle-aged woman who seemed more interested in my sex life than my emotional well-being. She, too, agreed that no parent and child bonding would take place. But she told me I was a lucky one. I was having a white child, and they were at a premium in Los Angeles. I wanted to ask questions, but my mother stood present at every meeting and shushed me when I opened my mouth to speak.

My sister talked about adopting the baby to keep it in the family, but then found out she was pregnant with her second. She couldn't take on two new kids, and soon became completely involved in her own pregnancy.

Steve cracked a piece out of my side bedroom window late one night. If anyone noticed it, I would say I stumbled and knocked the floor lamp into it. Steve wanted me to run away with him. We'd both be eighteen shortly after the baby was due, and then nobody could touch us. Steve had the band and I could go to work.

He'd just moved again and told the manager of the building his wife would be moving in within the week. When I explained that I was locked in, Steve asked what Mom had done. He couldn't believe I wasn't even able to use the bathroom at night; he was horrified by all of it. I could see he was getting agitated, like somebody on speed, and told him to calm down. He told me to stay awake until he returned. He was back in less than two hours with a ring of padlock keys. He told me to try them all, then and there. One, when wiggled around right, opened the door to the hall. I hid that key in my boot with my other valuables. I agreed to pack only what I absolutely needed to survive the first couple of weeks, and be ready to leave the minute Steve tapped on the window.

Chapter Fifteen

"Goodbye, Yellow Brick Road"
Sir Elton John

I sat up each night for two weeks, an old purse stashed on the shelf above my closet, jammed with essentials, waiting for Steve. After three weeks passed, I resigned myself to the fact that he'd changed his mind. When I dared, I unlocked the door to the hall and phoned Cathi, Katy, Rita, Joe. Cathi visited two or three times a week, and we whispered through the three-inch hole in my window. She knew I needed contact, unlike Jeanne who completely abandoned me. Jeanne wouldn't even take my calls.

I'd never had a drink, but needed something, badly. When I looked in the bathroom cupboard, Mom's Ten High was gone. She'd moved her stash. I tried taking a full bottle of aspirin, which only made me deathly ill and gave me a ripper headache. Mom told me I owed her a bottle of aspirin.

One night I started screaming. It was spontaneous and uncontrollable. I was told to shut up. My aunt wanted to phone the doctor, but Mom forbade her. The screaming was happening more and more often, and seemed to be disassociated from me; it had a life of its own. I must have had some unconscious control over it, because it only happened at night. Finally my father spent a long weekend soundproofing the garage. Every night I was led out there and locked in until eleven o'clock. I remember hearing myself scream. It was an agonized sound that reverberated inside my head.

I needed to make it all stop. Mom obviously knew I was having a psychological problem, because razor blades and other implements of destruction were removed from the bathroom. One afternoon, when the baby was kicking hard, I shoved a chair under the outside bathroom door and began slamming my head into the wall, over and over again. I regained consciousness to see a blurry image of my mother standing over me, shouting for me to get up. I couldn't lift my head. She left me on the floor until my father came home. He carried me to my bed and brought me ice wrapped in a washcloth. The next day I looked in the mirror to see one dilated pupil and another that looked like a pinpoint. The left side of my head was bruised and swollen. I was nauseated and had sickening, stabbing pains in my head. I knew I had a concussion, but it didn't matter. Nothing did.

The next time Cathi came to the window, I begged her to bring me drugs, and lots of them. I had to end the whole mess. Cathi wrote back that it wasn't my mess; my mother was crazy and cruel but within a few months it would all be over and I'd be free. In the meantime, Cathi was going to try to talk to her mother. She told me to hang in there; she'd come up with something.

Cathi started shoving joints through the hole in the window. I smoked them in the bathroom with the water running. My mother was so drunk she didn't know the difference between her cigarette smoke and my weed smoke.

One night Cathi brought me a pile of notes and cards that wouldn't fit through the hole in the window. I saw Charley's name, Joe's name, Cathy Costa's name; everybody was still out there. Cathi said the whole Strip knew and that she'd shove the good wishes under the gate. My mother got to them before I did. She had my father repair the hole in my window, install a spotlight that illuminated the gate all night every night, and ask Mrs. Stoddard to let Mom know if she saw anyone on the walkway.

The last message Cathi got through to me was a note from Steve. Cathi held it to the window and turned the pages as I read by flashlight. Steve explained he hadn't deserted me. My mother tried, several times, to have him arrested for coming by. The cops told her that as far as the law was concerned he was a young man of legal age attempting to visit, but that they could usher him off the property if she insisted, which she did. The next time she saw him start up the walkway, she had him arrested for breaking and entering, something he hadn't done. He wouldn't have dared for fear of exactly what happened, and that was jail time. Thankfully the cops didn't question Steve's I.D., and he was released after an inspector took a good look at the back door, which Steve had supposedly broken in. It was intact and the paint was old. My mother had been caught in her own lie. Steve begged Cathi to get the message to me, and she finally had. My mother saw Cathi leaving, and screamed at my father to "get rid of Sally." He took her by the shoulders, steered her into their bedroom, and the house was quiet the rest of the night.

The next morning Mom came into my room with a pair of scissors. Since I wasn't going anywhere, it was time to cut my hair. Yes, hair grew back, but she'd taken enough already and would get even more when my baby was born. I tried to twist the scissors from her hand, but damn she was strong when angry. She pressed the scissor points into the soft hollow at the base of my throat. I felt strangely calm because I was sure she was going to kill me, and I didn't care. After a long still moment, I looked into her unblinking eyes and saw an awful combination of terror, rage, and confusion, a look I wouldn't see on her face again until she lay paralyzed on her deathbed decades later. "You don't want to do this," I whispered to myself in amazement. She blinked once, dropped the scissors, and walked out.

That little padlock key, my one chance at freedom, stayed in the toe of my boot. I'd done something I never thought I'd do. I'd given up.

My water broke late one night. By the time I changed into dry clothes and got to the car, my mother was already riding shotgun. I was admitted to maternity and my mother told the nurse to anesthetize me. There was no natural childbirth in those days, and epidurals hadn't been invented. Women were laid on tables and given a nasty drug referred to as twilight sleep. I begged to stay fully awake, and the nurse said it was my right. My mother stomped out. Three minutes later, the nurse came back and jabbed a needle in my arm on doctor's orders. I shouted once. I yelled, "God, help me!" It was the last time I ever asked God for anything.

In the delivery room, I was blindfolded and my arms were tied to the table. No mother and child bonding was going to take place here. When my son was born early the next morning, I heard him cry and jerked up in an attempt to reach for him. A strong hand slammed me back down onto the table so hard it made my nose bleed and somebody said, "She's awake." The nurses must have seen the blood running from my nose to my mouth, because a female voice mentioned something about a brain hemorrhage. There was a jab in my upper arm. I heard that the baby was six pounds one ounce, and looked good and healthy. Then I was out cold.

Back at home, I stopped eating. Food, even water, made me sick. I was in awful pain. A week later, days before my eighteenth birthday, I was driven to the county adoption agency and signed away my rights as a mother. The papers included a special clause indicating that I would never attempt to find my son. I signed everything. The social worker put her arm around me and encouraged me to cry. I pushed her away. As I stood up to leave, a young man who had been working in the next room approached my social worker. "You're legally required to be sure she knows her rights," he said. The social worker hissed something at him, but he stood his ground.

I discovered I had the right to know about my son's adoptive parents. I learned their ages, educational backgrounds, and ethnicity. I had a right to a photo of my son. I asked for a copy. And I had the right to see him. I wanted to.

The baby was brought to me in a plain white blanket and felt incredibly warm in my arms. He fussed a little but looked healthy and beautiful. He had Steve's remarkable eyes. The young man ushered my parents into the room. My mother was furious. "You wanted to take him away; here he is," I said, thrusting the baby into her arms. My son started screaming. Mom quickly handed him to my father, and the baby immediately calmed down.

As we were leaving, the young man hurried to catch up with us. He took me by the shoulder and told me he hoped I hadn't been cajoled into giving away my son; every mother had the legal right to keep her own child, no matter what her age or situation. He trusted that I'd been offered county assistance so I could support the baby until I got a job. There was screaming inside my head. I kept asking, "What?! What?! What?!" because the answers didn't make sense. I'd been lied to and conspired against by my parents, my doctor, and my government-employed social worker. For some unknown reason, Pat Boone's lie about the Las Vegas Beatle party flashed through my mind. The young man asked if I was all right. Although I couldn't breathe, some part of me decided to get it together and move on. I looked into those honest, concerned eyes and said everything was fine. Then I climbed in the back seat of my father's car. On the way home, my mother started fussing about my father's driving. I said, "If you can't shut up for once in your life, just let me out of the car now. If you won't pull over, I'll jump." We were on the back side of the winding road that led to the top of the hill, and a good jump from a moving car would have taken me over the edge of the cliff. Both of my parents stayed silent for the rest of the drive.

Steve phoned. It sounded like a long-distance call. His voice echoed, and I could tell somebody else was on the line. He said he only had a minute, so I told him the baby had been a boy and gave him what few details I knew about the adoptive parents. He asked if I was okay, and I said I thought I was sick. He started to respond and the line went dead. I later learned that Ordinary Men had broken up and the members had joined other groups. Nobody had seen Steve for a couple of months. I never heard from him again.

Friends phoned, asking why I hadn't moved out as planned. I had trouble talking to them. Something was wrong. I had a lot of abdominal pain and often couldn't even keep down water. Sometimes the pain took my breath away. But when I said anything to the family, I was told to shut up.

Exactly one month after giving birth, I was doubled over on the sofa in tears. My mother put a plate of food in front of me. The sight and smell of it made me sick. I pushed it away.

The pain got worse. The vision in my right eye went dark. Most of the pain was localized in my lower right side and my legs were numb. By midnight I could only take little gulps of air. I crawled into my parents' room and said I was sick, that something was wrong. My mother told me to shut up and go to sleep. Her Ten High stench made me gag.

I begged my aunt to call the doctor. My mother instructed her to leave me alone. Finally I convinced Es to pull the phone to the door of my room. I couldn't reach far enough to dial. My mother got up and asked my aunt to go ahead and phone Dr. Baird. He didn't think I had a serious problem, but warned my mother not to let me lie on my right side, just in case. She immediately turned me onto my right side, which cut off my breathing completely. My father pulled on street clothes and said he was taking me to the emergency room. My mother coldly directed him to get back into bed. He did.

In the morning my aunt and my father both left for work, but my sister stopped by. She took one look at me and said she was taking me to the hospital. She instructed my mother to phone the doctor. He told Mom to bring me to his house. My mother prodded me up the flight of stairs to his front door. When Dr. Baird saw me, he yelled, "Margaret! I told you not to let Sally set foot on a stair!" He helped me back down the stairs and followed us to the hospital.

Still five foot nine, I weighed in at eighty-eight pounds. Before I passed out, I called Cathi's house and reached her father. He promised to let Cathi know where I was.

The next three days were a blur. Dr. Baird visited every day, and on that third afternoon he told me he figured I probably had an infection related to the childbirth, and he wanted to send me home. I buzzed for the nurse, declared that I was eighteen years old, had Dr. Baird removed as my physician, and asked for somebody else, anybody else.

That night, a young doctor, Gene Kaufmann, came to see me. As he began a pelvic exam I heard a horrible blood-curdling scream that shook the bed. It had come from me. The girl in the bed next to me cried, "Oh God, do something for her! I've been watching her die for three days and I can't stand it anymore!" Dr. Kaufmann had me prepped for emergency surgery.

My appendix had ruptured that first night, and I had peritonitis all through my abdominal cavity. I woke up long enough to see my parents at the foot of the bed before I passed out from the pain. When I woke again, I realized I was hooked to a stomach pump and had IVs in both arms, both legs, and my neck. I couldn't open my eyes, but I could hear a man tell my parents that I wouldn't live until morning and they'd better make funeral arrangements. For the first and only time in my life, I heard my father sob.

It was a dingy twenty-bed inter-community hospital, and I was in a dim little isolation room at the end of the hall. As soon as I got a staph infection, which was "inevitable," I was dead. And staph was highly contagious, so those who entered my room wore protective gear.

The stomach pump tube was moved farther into my intestines several times a day. After about a week, I could turn my head enough to see the ten-foot mark. When I could get words out, I begged the staff to let me die.

Gail came by. She bounced into the room chattering about how Cathi had the flu, took one look at me, and started crying. She said she was terribly sorry I was so sick, and quickly left. A few days later Willy walked through my door with a bunch of wildflowers. He looked at me and choked. He couldn't get his breath. A nurse took him away, and someone put the flowers in a jar in a corner of the room.

One afternoon, Charley showed up with a stack of good wishes from the Hollywood crowd. When he saw the tubes, needles, blood-stained sheets, and matted hair, he started teasing me. They were terrible jokes. "There's a swell invention called a hairbrush, you know." "I never figured you for S & M." "If you don't like it here, get up and walk out; I'll drive." I kept asking him to leave, but he refused. That night we watched *The Smother's Brothers Comedy Hour* together. Tommy was doing a frog prince bit, and I found myself laughing, gagging on the stomach pump tube. That just seemed to strike Charley funny, because he continued making bad jokes. I remember choking on tears and telling him how badly I wanted to die. He told me I was going to walk out of that hospital and get my skinny ass back to the Strip, where I belonged.

I woke up in the morning. It was the first time I actually woke up from sleep since I'd been admitted to the hospital over three weeks before. The nurses gathered around my bed. My favorite nurse, Evelyn, told me my fever had broken and I was going to be all right. By the end of the week, all tubes and needles were removed. My aunt said Jeanne was coming to visit and wanted to bring something. I didn't have a phone in my room, but there was a pay phone down the hall. I told my aunt to ask Jeanne to bring a roll of dimes and a pizza.

The next day, Willy returned with a clay pot filled with straw flowers. Rita showed up. She said Dinah, cousin to Dan of Warpath, was just down the hall with new pins in a badly broken leg. Dinah and I began sending notes to each other. She'd gone to South High too, but was older, so we'd never met. It really was a small world.

Warpath was a newer rock group made up of Native Americans. One day Dinah sent Dan up the hall to visit "the girl who almost died." I'd gotten permission to wash my hair two days before, and was wearing eye makeup and a funky pink nightshirt. Dan looked like a stereotypical Indian, complete with suede-sheathed knife on his belt. What made his appearance remarkable was very long, stick straight, naturally white-blond hair. We just stared at each other. He asked me when I was going to be released from the hospital. Dinah, whose father was long deceased and whose mother had died the year before, was going to stay with him while she healed. Did I want to visit? He had a place in the Hollywood hills.

Chapter Sixteen

"She's Leaving Home, Bye Bye"
The Beatles

On the way home from the hospital, my father asked if there was anything I wanted. Apparently a now-ill Mrs. Crane had spoken to my parents about their behavior toward me. I "wanted" the maw of hell to ingest them both, but I simply asked to drive through Jack in the Box for fries and a chocolate shake. I had to change the dressing on my incision for another couple of weeks and rest for the next month, and I was going to make the best of it. But as soon as we were home, Mom sat me down and told me I was going to enroll in college and get a job, now, seeping wound and all. I told her I'd begin making calls, grabbed the Classifieds, emptied the chocolate shake into the sink, and took the phone into my grandmother's room.

Dinah told me to come stay at Dan's. He didn't live alone; there were about a dozen people there, and everyone was cool. Dinah was still on crutches, but she'd begun babysitting for working mothers. Daycare didn't exist yet, and a whole new generation of women was taking jobs, so business was great. Would I be willing to help her? I asked Dinah to check with Dan, who said he'd pick me up.

I couldn't drive for another month, so Dan showed up in his bright red truck with a "Custer Died For Your Sins" sticker on the rear bumper. His brother, Dennis, and his brother's girlfriend, Sue, were with him, ready to drive the Nash up to Hollywood. I'd ride with Dan. When the group entered the house, my mother demanded to know what was going on. I picked up my acoustic guitar, handed Dan my portable stereo, and snatched up my shoulder bag. "I'm leaving," I said. "You've got a ten o'clock curfew!" she shouted. Dan, Dennis, Sue, and I gaped at each other. I was eighteen years old, I'd given birth to a child, and recently had almost died, and this woman was trying to give me a curfew.

"No," I corrected her, "I'm leaving. I'm not coming back." I heard her wrists smack the doorframe as she flung out her arms to block my exit. "You can't do this; I won't permit it!" she shrieked. "And you certainly won't take anything from my house," she added in an unearthly wail. "I paid for these things," I told her. "You just go ahead and keep everything else."

I wanted to slap her good, just once, but knew I'd go to jail for it. So I quietly walked past her and climbed into Dan's truck. We drove Dennis and Sue to my car. I let Lynn know I was moving it elsewhere and thanked her for letting me park on the street all that time. She'd heard what had happened and wished me luck. It took a quick jump to get that old Nash running, but once it was going, it was good. Dennis and Sue waved at us and we drove off into the future.

Dan's girlfriend no longer lived with him. They'd been fighting and decided to cool it for awhile. That left room for me. There were four bedrooms and one nasty little bathroom. Weeds grew from the shower drain. The floors were unfinished cement. Furniture was, at best, eclectic. But there was a huge living room and kitchen, perfect for babysitting. Out back there was an enormous garage the size of a warehouse where the guys sometimes rehearsed. Around the side was an unattached room with glass doors. We guessed it might have been a greenhouse. Dan hadn't been living there long, and apologized for the condition of the place. I promised that as soon as I could get around better, I'd paint the floors, clean up the garden, and make things look more appropriate. Sue agreed to help. I knew I was going to love her.

There were other household members, people who sometimes stayed and other times disappeared for days on end. Dan, Dennis, Sue, Dinah, and I were the primary breadwinners and housekeepers. Dan had gigs and would eventually go on tours. Dennis worked at a machine shop. Sue had been caring for an elderly woman who was being moved to a care facility; she asked if she could help Dinah and me with babysitting. Within a month, the living room and kitchen looked like something out of the fifties, and the bathroom was painted and made as tolerable as possible. But our spaces, the bedrooms, all were painted black. We hung posters and black lights, and one night Dan came home with four lava lamps. The yard was looking good, and Dan bought a lawn mower so he wouldn't have to keep borrowing from the neighbors. The marijuana in the canister on top of the fridge stayed put. No child would ever be able to reach it. And heavier drugs were only done at night, once our little charges had been picked up by their parents.

Sue was an earth mother. Although she was seriously overweight, she looked cuddly rather than fat. Her hair was long and dark, and she had huge blue eyes. People trusted her. Dinah carried a lot of weight around her middle due to some disease I never truly understood. She had thigh-length light brown hair, the shiniest hair I'd ever seen. And Dinah sang, beautifully. She put Katy to shame. Dinah had sung in her church choir as a child, was taught operatic voice at an early age, and could create a beautiful Joan Baez vibrato or a down-and-dirty Grace Slick or Janis Joplin. Both Sue and Dinah took it upon themselves to feed me constantly. They wanted me back up to my normal 110 pounds.

We mimeographed babysitting service fliers and word spread. Yes, working wives and scandalous single mothers could leave their kids with three trustworthy young women during the day. We charged on a sliding scale and did freebies for girls we knew couldn't pay. In some cases we bartered, accepting homemade bread, car repairs, and other trade-offs. We wanted to pull our weight, but we didn't need to support the entire household. Dennis brought in minimum wage and Dan made decent money with his gigs. It worked out well.

At night the place got crowded, although we were careful to keep noise to a minimum during the work week. Not only did we want to avoid a bust, we wanted to be courteous. After all, we were children of the forties. We'd been raised that way.

About two weeks after moving into Dan's, Rita picked me up to take me to Laurel Canyon. We stopped and saw Frank Zappa, who'd heard I'd been sick and genuinely seemed concerned about my well-being. I loved Frank. Everybody loved Frank. Nobody was around at Joe's place; I'd have to ask Cathi if the guys had moved. The Whiskey was busy. We sat near the back, and Rita struck up a conversation with Lee, who'd played with Country Joe and the Fish and a couple of other bands. He was loud and everything seemed to strike him funny. Lee was with a friend, a cutie-pie type named Paul. At about midnight, the four of us left in Rita's car.

The guys were staying at a house in West L.A. It was very nouveau riche chic. Lee unlocked the security door, and then opened the front door. A dark-haired woman was asleep on the sofa, so we went into the kitchen. It reminded me of a fifties diner but was much more elegant. There was a circular booth in the center and a lazy Susan full of drugs sat in the center of the table. What did we want? Paul said they usually didn't do speed at night, and Rita told him that was fine, because I couldn't handle speed of any kind. She remembered the time I'd taken a couple of whites and went into tachycardia. She and Connie had to keep me flat on my back, trying to breathe steadily, all night long. So Lee held out two reds. Seconal was a serious sleeping pill.

I figured two reds would knock me out, and considering how bad my insomnia had been the last year, that sounded good. But they didn't knock me out; instead, they just made me stupid.

Suddenly everything was funny. And apparently I was funny, because I seemed to be cracking everybody else up. I remember being in bed with Lee, and sex not hurting at all despite the recent surgery. I remember telling him that the name "Lee" seriously did not suit him. And I desperately tried to convince him to get a gig with Cream because he looked right for the group.

In the morning we all went out for breakfast. We ate everything on the table, mostly with our fingers, and laughed so loud the manager of the café threatened us twice. I didn't care. I was having fun, something that hadn't happened in a very long time.

Back at Dan's, Dinah introduced us to a new guy she'd met. His name was Don and he taught guitar. Dinah seemed completely taken with him, and Don soon became another fixture around the house. He didn't work a nine-to-five, but there were enough rock star wannabes around to keep him in cash.

Vegetarianism was a house rule, and I was more than fine with that. I'd never liked the idea of meat. Susie started a vegetable garden and a compost vat. We provided regular babysitting on weekdays, but kept weekends for ourselves. Dennis typically worked six in the morning until two in the afternoon. And Dan worked whatever hours his gigs required. We'd become a nice little group.

Chapter Seventeen

"Hollywood Nights"
Bob Seger

Cathi phoned. Her mother had died in the middle of the night. After bursting into tears myself, I phoned Gail. She'd already talked to Rob, Cathi's latest love and a guy I'd known since kindergarten. Dan walked in and asked what was going on. I asked if he'd go with us to the funeral. It was the one time he left his knife at home.

I was surprised to see that Gail was happily pregnant. Her boyfriend, who had a very low draft number, was in Canada for the week, finding a place for them to live. I wouldn't be seeing her for awhile, so between the death of Mrs. Willard and Gail leaving, it was a somber day.

Cathi phoned again a couple of weeks later. She'd gotten her hands on some exclusive weed and wanted me to try it. It was cut with something; she wasn't sure what. So Dennis, Sue, Dan, and I drove down to the beach to pick up Cathi's gift.

Dumb luck got us home safely, because all I remember is lying on the grass in the front yard, looking at nude dead bodies hanging from the telephone poles. I wasn't afraid; I was fascinated. A guy who was spending the night asked for a couple of tokes, and promptly put his fist through the window of his car, something none of us would completely comprehend until the next day when we saw his bruised and blood-crusted hand and the hole in his passenger side window. Toward morning, somebody suggested that we visit Rita, who was still seventeen and obligated to live at home. Her mother was gone, and she had three guys in her bedroom. I woke up on her living room floor with a backache. Dan was asleep next to me, his remarkable hair fanned out across my naked midsection. Apparently we'd had sex. I hoped it had been good.

I started going to Dan's gigs. His band had a different sound. They weren't screaming rockers but they weren't folk. They sang ballads with a rock edge before "folk-rock" became an accepted term. The music was advertised as controversial because it addressed the war, civil rights, and the plight of the American Indian. Gigs allowed me to see a different side of Dan. He mixed frightening combinations of drugs before going on stage: Psilocybin, speed, mescaline. And lots of acid. And when stoned, he was mean. Managers everywhere gossiped about his attitude and how to deal with it. I started thinking Warpath might be in trouble and wondered how safe I was living in Dan's house.

My old energy was back, and it was time to reassess my life. I couldn't stay at Dan's forever, and most of my girlfriends were living with guys. Gail was moving to Canada. Don told me he was going to ask Dinah to marry him. Cheryl was living with a guy at the beach. Connie had moved to Haight-Ashbury and would soon be followed by Katy. Rita was stuck at home for now. Cathi was in transition; her mother's death put her in a bad space. She had just moved nearby, selling the Free Press for rent money. Jeanne was going to USC but living at home, where we all figured she'd eventually die of old age. And Sue had just confided to me that she thought she was pregnant; I knew she and Dennis were destined to get married and I was happy for her.

I spent a lot of time sitting on the dirt floor of the shower, lukewarm water running down my back. I was mad. I was mad at the crap I'd been through, I was mad at Joe (the one man I still couldn't let go of), and I was mad at myself.

All that thinking about Joe brought him back into my life again. Within a week, Cathy Costa and Rita both phoned me with information. They'd heard, from separate sources, that Joe had taken three of my songs, set them to his own music, and recorded them. When I tried to reach Joe, however, I ended up talking to someone who was housesitting. The guy said he'd leave a note for Joe, but I never got a call.

After seeing Dan high on homemade concoctions, I started driving him to his gigs. Once he was inside the venue and had gotten stoned, I left. For several months I slept with any musician with a recording contract, but it had to be a major contract. And the guys needed to be headliners, because anything less was a waste of time. I popped reds or yellows on weekends and smoked a lot of weed. I was trying to get back into the Canyon girl head, but it wasn't working.

This new lifestyle wore thin very quickly. I turned the babysitting business over to Dinah and Sue, and signed on as an office worker with three temp agencies. One personnel director, Donna McGovern, became a casual friend. We talked over lunch several times, and spilled our respective guts. When she learned about my situation, she promised to get me work, anywhere in Southern California, on a day's notice. She stayed true to her word for the next six years.

Katy phoned. We hadn't seen each other in almost a year. I told her to come on over. She was a mess. She'd "lost" her car and had been hitchhiking. The first thing she did was vomit on the living room floor, which made her laugh hysterically. Then she decided she wanted to color with some Crayons left on the coffee table from the day's babysitting. She broke one Crayon in half and ate it. When she started choking I got her some water, which she immediately spilled all over the music I'd been writing. Her pupils were dilated, and her movements were jerky. She'd taken something that had affected her nervous system and couldn't remember what it was. I was the only one home, and I couldn't handle her; she had a good twenty-five pounds on me. So I piled her into the car and went in search of help.

I asked at the major clubs and discovered Charley working at a new, smaller, semi-exclusive club. He was glad to see me. Was I okay? Could he do anything for me? Where was I staying? I said I had a problem and dragged Katy out of the car. Charley said, "Oh shit," and took her into the club.

Katy was out of control and started taking punches at Charley and me. Then she began vomiting again. She was laughing at the same time, which made her choke. Charley did the only thing he could think of. He slapped her, then stuck his fingers down her throat until she threw up again. Each time she started to laugh, he slapped her again. It took about ten minutes of wrestling with her before she was empty and beginning to sober up. By the time Charley declared her "safe," the club had closed.

Katy was sleeping with a married man. She lived with the guy's best friend, so when her lover wanted to see her, he simply told his wife he was visiting his friend. Clever. The house wasn't too far away, and Charley, knowing how upset and tired I was, called a friend to drive Katy home. I had her promise to call me in the morning but didn't expect anything. I'd heard that Katy was into heavy drug use and planned to move to Haight-Ashbury.

Charley had handled Katy so well and thought nothing of it. I'd known him for years now, and he was solid as a rock, always there, but behind the scenes. I thanked him profusely and gave him a quick kiss goodbye. He said, "If you ever need to escape, just let me know." I stopped and reached out my hand. He took it. I led him into the back, found an office, and gently pushed him down on a sofa. He gave me an odd smile. Then he got to his knees in good, old-fashioned Charley style, and took off his shirt. Those skinny hips, a surprisingly cut chest, and all that unruly hair suddenly seemed very sexy. He pulled my top off over my head without even tangling a curl, yanked down my jeans, and started biting my stomach. I said, "What are you doing?" and he laughed.

"I don't know," he said, unbuttoning his own jeans, "but I'm sure I'll think of something."

He was one of the most talented men I ever slept with. Not only did he have skill and technique, he was an artist. He was one of those rare guys who wants to please while having a hell of a good time himself. If I hadn't been such a psychological and emotional wreck, I would have hung onto Charley. We had one night of incredible sex, with him telling me he'd loved me since we first met. But in the morning light, he was Charley my buddy again. He wasn't going to push it. It's one of the things that made him special.

At the house, Dan was awake. He asked where I'd been. I explained about Katy; she was high on something, and I'd taken her to a friend who knew how to deal with bad trips. Dan accepted the story, but he had an odd look on his face. I didn't like it. But I also knew, at that point in my life, I didn't want to live alone.

Chapter Eighteen

"You Say It's Time We Move in Together"
Carly Simon

I went into denial. I stopped going to Dan's gigs. I took as many office jobs as I could cram into any given week. And I spent most nights in Dan's bed, just to be close to someone.

Dan had a low draft number and was getting scared. He sat me down one day and asked if I wanted to get married. I had no desire to marry him; he frightened me and I certainly didn't love him. But he kept pushing the issue. He had taken me in when I'd needed it, so I felt like I had to do something to help. He tried to get conscientious objector status from the draft, but nobody would back him up. Rob had a C.O., and Gary got one, but they were sincere. Neither of them would have ever picked up a gun. Despite Warpath's anti-war songs, Dan actually believed we should "get those gooks." I hadn't known this before, and it made me feel sick. I was glad I'd kept my political activities to myself. I didn't want to get into it with Dan.

The lower his number dropped, the more upset Dan got about being drafted. Several of us suggested he move to Canada. I offered to hook him up with Gail and Ross; they'd found a place out in the sticks where they were living safely and happily. But Dan was pushing the idea of marriage. It was easier than moving out of the country and would allow him to continue with Warpath. I wished he hadn't played the music card, because his passion for creating great songs was the one thing I respected about him. I wanted Dan and Warpath to be able to continue to make their unique music.

I suggested to Dan that we get a fake marriage license and see if the draft board would accept it, but he wasn't willing to take the risk. Later in the day when I was alone, I phoned Tina Van Voorhees. After I explained the situation, she told me to take Dan to Tijuana, go to the American Consul, get a marriage license, and tell Dan we were married. As long as I could avoid an actual wedding, and if I was careful to never register the license in the United States, Dan would have a convincing piece of paper and I'd still be single. Tina told me the Mexican marriage license trick had worked for several people she knew, and trusted it would work for me. I just had to convince Dan. I called Cathi and she dissolved in laughter. Cheryl and her boyfriend had just conned the draft board with a Tijuana marriage license.

Dan loved drugs, so I decided to get him very stoned, take him to Mexico, have a marriage license drawn up, and tell him we were married. The draft board had accepted Cheryl and David's marriage license, so they'd probably accept ours.

Cathi wanted to go to Mexico this time; this was too fun to miss. So Cathi, Dennis, a pregnant Sue, Dan, and I crammed ourselves into that old blue station wagon that had belonged to Mrs. Willard, and headed for the border. Once there, I suggested to Dan that we get married. In Mexico we didn't even need a blood test. The American Consul sent us to a man with acceptable English skills. Cathi distracted Dennis and Sue with a wedding ring hunt (six bucks for a decent silver ring), and Dan and I filled out the necessary forms. They were long, and entirely in Spanish. When the man said, "You're done," I kissed Dan and said, "We can leave, sweetheart." He thought we were married. All the way home that night Dan bragged that the draft wouldn't get him now. Cathi couldn't stop laughing.

In the sober light of day, Dan began having second thoughts. What if being married wasn't enough? He wanted me to get pregnant. There was screaming in my head again, but I simply said, "That would be nice, if it happened." Dan went into the bathroom and I pulled on my work slacks. When Dan returned, he had my diaphragm in his hand. He'd sliced it in half.

Despite the fact that I panicked, called Donna, explained I'd be about two hours late to work, and got a new diaphragm that morning, six weeks later I was confirmed pregnant. I didn't know much about American Indian rituals and was actually superstitious, thinking that Dan had somehow manifested this baby. Diaphragms were considered reliable birth control. After serious consideration, I decided I wanted the child. I realized it could, in reality, have been Charley's (which made me smile) or even the child of one of the other guys I'd been with during the past few months, but the due date was specific. This baby was Dan's.

Once Dan had a doctor's note verifying my pregnancy, he sent it along with our "marriage license" to the draft board. And when he got word he was safe from the draft, he became easier to live with. He got everybody together to discuss living arrangements. Dennis and Sue were getting married soon and were already looking for a place. Dinah and Don were getting married too and were going to stay with Don's sister for awhile. Dan decided to give up the house and told me to start looking for a place. God, I didn't want to live alone with him.

I found an apartment building not far from the Strip. The units were connected and just one level. There was a communal yard in the center and decent parking both out front and in the back. We moved in the next month.

Dan came home angry one night, just a week after we'd moved. The gig hadn't gone well. Although I'd been home all evening, he accused me of cheating on him and he shoved me. Hard. I warned him that I was pregnant and that if I lost the baby, he'd lose his government daddy-to-be status and be drafted. I added I would not stay married to him if he brought drugs into the apartment. Even weed was forbidden. I was keeping this baby, and I was taking good care of it.

Dan didn't want me to work. During the mid-to-late sixties, pregnant women typically didn't work, so his request wasn't unusual, but the day after he'd told me to stay home and take care of myself, I heard him talking to Hawk, his equipment manager and slimiest buddy. Dan wanted me indebted to him, "without possible means of escape." Time shifted and I was right back in that locked room at my parents' house. When Dan left that night I phoned Donna at home. Within three days she found me a four-hour-a-day job that would last about three months. I told no one. While Dan slept, I got dressed, drove about three miles, and made out invoices and answered phones in a back office, typically returning before Dan even woke up. I kept my overnight bag in the Nash, and changed from baggy pregnancy jeans to a maternity skirt in the restroom at work. In the evenings when Dan had a gig, I visited Charley. We played Monopoly, and both cheated. The best times of my pregnancy were those evenings with Charley. The couple of times Dan came home early or woke up while I was gone, I told him I'd stopped at the store. I carried the same shopping bag of Prell shampoo around for three months, in case I needed proof. Dan remained tolerable during the rest of my pregnancy.

On a sunny April afternoon, I got into the car, started the engine, and, as always, turned on the radio. As I headed to a meeting with Donna, the disc jockey announced that Martin Luther King Jr. had been assassinated in Memphis. I slammed on the brakes, as did two people on the other side of the road. I recognized one driver as a neighbor. He shouted, "Did you just hear that?" and I yelled back. A half dozen of us pulled over, got out of our cars, and sat down on the sidewalk. We'd lost the one black man who was peacefully promoting civil rights. That night there was a makeshift candlelight vigil. Nobody slept.

Two months later, Dan and I were watching the news. Bobby Kennedy, our hope for change in America, was talking at the Ambassador Hotel downtown, that great place I'd met a couple of the Stones and other musicians. Suddenly the camera angles shifted and we could only see the back of the crowd. The newscaster said, "Bobby Kennedy has been shot." I jumped up and screamed, "That's not funny!" I couldn't believe it was happening; I thought it was a bad joke. I screamed, "That's not funny!" again, and Dan took my arm and sat me down. Bobby was lying on the floor, and Rosie Grier grabbed Sirhan Sirhan, holding him for the police. Bobby was alive. He was taken to a local hospital where he underwent brain surgery.

None of us slept that night. We phoned each other, remembering when John Kennedy was shot just a few years earlier. The next morning we learned that Bobby hadn't made it. Our hope for the future was literally dead.

Martin Luther King Jr. and Bobby Kennedy had been assassinated within two months of each other. Something had gone wrong with the world my child was going to be born into.

Cathi phoned. She was back in town after a trip, and her familiar criticisms sounded like a love song. She'd landed a job with an accountant and was living about ten miles from my place. Cathi wanted to give me a late birthday gift; it was a backstage pass to the Doors concert at the Hollywood Bowl, something I wasn't about to miss. I phoned Ann and coerced her into calling the apartment while Dan was home. She told him she needed a babysitter for just one night and couldn't reach her regular girl. Dan passed along the information, and I groaned that I really couldn't turn her down. I tried to keep my excitement to a minimum, but Dan asked what I was up to. Having just seen the doctor for my monthly visit, I explained that pregnant women went through some strange hormonal changes and that one day he might find me laughing, the next day crying. It had been a long time since I'd seen a major concert, and Dan wasn't going to ruin it for me.

The Doors had been local for awhile, and just recently hit it big. Their first album was an immediate success, and they would be touring Europe soon. As Cathi said, West Coast boys made good again. I'd met Jim Morrison in L.A. years earlier. I remembered him as a short-haired pudgy little twerp I snubbed, but knew from recent photos he'd completely changed his image. Charley knew several of Jim's old college friends, who swore he was an absolute fake, a guy who wanted to create a fortune in filmmaking but jumped on the music bandwagon the first chance he had. Obviously Charley didn't like Jim.

The Doors music was remarkable. Jim must have developed a passion for it; if he hadn't, it was one hell of a facade, because I knew passion-driven music when I heard it. I had no idea what to expect backstage and hoped Jim wouldn't remember me and my past snobbery.

The place was jammed. Apparently half of Los Angeles had a pass. But Cathi managed to lead me through the crowd to meet the guys. It was like a receiving line, with handshakes and how-do-you-dos. An older guy handed me a joint right in front of one of the security cops, who didn't bat an eye. I was having a good time, but that initial blast of excitement was gone. I was taking a hit of weed when I spotted one of the Doors weaving his way through the crowd. He singled me out. He grinned and asked if I was pregnant. I was wearing regular jeans, slightly loose but acceptable, a long-sleeved shirt and a poncho. I didn't show much yet and wondered how he knew. "I can smell it," he smiled, "it's the best scent in the world." The conversation didn't go unheard. Four other girls there were also pregnant and let it be known. Apparently pregnant women turned this guy on, and I was the only one who didn't know about the fetish. He rather rudely dismissed the other girls, told me I was something special, then rattled off several questions regarding marital status, love-relationship situation, and so forth. Seemingly satisfied, he asked me back to his place after the show. I went.

He treated me with what can only be described as reverence. He was gentle and took things slow and easy. He loved the fact that I was lactating and that he could feel the baby kick. For somebody with a down-and-dirty image, a guy who could have slept with just about anyone anytime, he had chosen me for a night of surprising tenderness.

During our next Monopoly game, Charley asked about the concert. I told him it was a good time, and he got quiet. In the middle of his next turn, he stopped, poured himself half a glass of whiskey, and swallowed it in one gulp. "You slept with him, didn't you?" he asked. I said, "Who?" and he gave me a look that shut me up. "Okay, yes," I confessed, suddenly feeling absolutely terrible for upsetting one of my best friends. It was the only time I saw Charley angry. "You're too good for him!" he shouted, slamming the Monopoly board shut, sending plastic hotels and fake money all over the floor.

I waited, scared stiff, for a solid five minutes before approaching Charley from the back. I knew what anger meant; it was typically followed by physical violence. I reached out a tentative hand to touch Charley's arm, when he turned and grabbed me. As usual in times of terror, I couldn't breathe. "Take care of things up here!" he shouted to a colleague, before dragging me into a small room at the back, a place I hadn't seen before. He laid two of his jackets on what was once a piece of lawn furniture, and laid me on my back. I stayed silent while he tore off his clothes and then did the same with mine. I managed to squeak out the words, "Please don't hurt the baby," which brought Charley to a dead halt. "Hurt it? I wanted it to be mine, damn it! When you told me your due date, I thought maybe it was. I've always wanted you," he said with tears in his eyes "It's always been you." And he made love to me, an expression not yet used for having romantic, gentle sex. When I left, early in the morning, I looked Charley square in the eye and said, "I love you." And I meant it, in every sense of the word. Dan was sound asleep when I got home. I spent the next week crying.

Angela was born on a foggy night, just before 10:00. I'd heard about natural childbirth but couldn't find a hospital willing to provide that option. So I insisted on no drugs (epidurals hadn't been invented) and used Yogic breathing to keep myself in control. After that awful first childbirth, this was easy. Angie was premature. The doctor had told me she was "in position" when I was eight months along, and as I feared, I didn't get to hold her. She spent that first week in an incubator. When she was ready to come home, Dan soberly drove and I held Angie close all the way.

I took Angie to the club so Charley could meet her, but the guys told me he'd taken a leave of absence. Somebody handed me an address in the Haight-Ashbury district, but added that his own attempts at contact went unreturned.

During the first few months, Dan played regular gigs and I taught Yoga. Angie was a terrific baby. I could pack her up and take her anywhere. Once she started to get active, I put cardboard boxes on the floor between the front and back seats of the Nash, covered the entire area with blankets, and filled the space with pillows, toys, crackers, and changes of clothing. If I was tired and Dan was playing, I'd go to a drive-in movie and let Angie fall asleep in the back.

The No Drugs rule stayed intact for almost a year. Then one day I came home to a coffee table littered with pills of every shape, size, and color. An older guy was sitting in my favorite chair, flipping through a fat roll of bills. Dan was buying and selling in the living room, and Angie was there to see it. When the guy left, I told Dan to get the drugs off the table and out of the apartment. He dumped the pills into a bag and overturned the stone-topped table, which broke into a dozen pieces.

Shortly after that, Dan started hitting me. Hard. Every time I called the cops, they came out to find me bruised, bleeding, and sobbing. Dan could maintain under pressure and always appeared absolutely cool, so the cops invariably asked what I did to provoke him. It was still all right to give your wife a black eye and busted lip in the sixties, and the one cop who actually seemed concerned about me said I'd have to go into the police station to file a report against Dan, and I'd have to do it every time he hit me. Dan wouldn't be arrested because women were still chattel, but the incidents would go on his record.

Once I'd been hit a dozen times, I decided to leave. Dan must have sensed something was up, because one morning he held me down and asked me what I was planning. Then he pulled out a bootlace (he wore knee-high moccasins), doubled it over, and choked me until I passed out. When I woke up, Angie was crying and my neck was burned and bleeding. I tried to open the front door and call to a neighbor, but the doors and windows had all been nailed shut with four-inchers. I phoned Larry and Greg, a gay couple who had become good friends. Larry came over, broke down the front door, and took Angie and me home with him.

During the Summer of Love, Dan and another member of Warpath decided to take a break from the band and travel, ending up at Woodstock. This decision lead to Warpath's ultimate demise. Sue had, by now, had a second child and wanted to leave Dennis. She and I agreed to move in together. We found an apartment farther inland, again off of Sunset. And when Warpath left, so did we.

After we got ourselves and the three kids settled into the new apartment, Sue and I decided to take a break, so we went with Larry and Greg to a love-in at Griffith Park. We let the kids run with the other toddlers for a while, until we saw an obese female member of a newly-famous music group giving tongue depressor licks of acid to everyone, including children. We reined in the kids and decided that from now on, we'd join love-ins on our own. Love-ins went on our No Kids Allowed list along with social/political protests and heavy drugs.

It was a beautiful summer. I carried just enough of a work load to get by, and Sue babysat weekdays. There was a shared, central water heater, so we managed with just electricity, no gas. The kids were still on toddler food, which we heated in the jar under hot running water. Sue and I cooked in a secondhand electric pot (the precursor of the crockpot), and survived on pasta or brown rice with vegetables. When we could afford to splurge, we tossed sweet-and-sour sauce on top. Sue found an enormous box of Lipton's at a swap meet, so there was always a pitcher of iced tea in the fridge. The kids had a good time in the playground downstairs, and Sue and I learned to make our own fun. We spent evenings watching our fourth-hand sound-free TV with the record player going. We entertained ourselves making up stories to go along with the combination of sight and sound.

The United States landed a man on the moon. I propped Angie in her toddler seat in front of the TV and tried to explain what was happening. Once it was dark out, I took her outside and told her to look at the moon; there were men walking on it. She didn't understand. I just wanted her to be able to tell her own children she'd seen the first manned moon landing.

Things were looking up for the world, and the flower children of the West Coast were celebrating. People were passing out weed on the street corners. We didn't worry too much about narcs, because at the time you could identify even the best undercover cops by their shoes; even if the shoes were appropriate to the outfit, they were always too new, never worn down at the heel. And Garry, a new neighbor, brought us hash. He was sixteen, his mother was never home, and he made a really nice living teaching people to roller skate; he worked with a local roller derby and was amazingly business minded. When Garry had new stuff for us, he'd knock at the door (which we didn't answer until the caller identified him/herself) and say, "It's just the wind." We called him Garry the Wind.

Yes, we broke our own house rule of No Drugs, but we were careful. We only got buzzed when the kids were in their room, asleep. And we never filled the house with smoke; we used our bedroom, which opened onto a balcony. We kept our stash in the ceiling of Sue's Ford. It barely ran and was parked around back where nobody bothered it.

Just two or three weeks after the moon landing, we heard about the Manson murders, and the celebrating stopped. Manson had really done it this time. People in the canyons heightened security on their homes. Club managers suggested people walk to their cars in groups. We were justifiably paranoid.

I ran into Jim of the Whispers at the supermarket. We'd met about three years prior, and recognized each other immediately. Jim was hard to miss at six foot six. He was in good shape, his hair had gone from Beatle length to mid-back, and his skin was deeply tanned. He asked what was new, and I told him I had a daughter. Jim wanted to meet her, so I told him to come for dinner.

The Whispers had produced a couple of records but hadn't gotten much radio time. People loved their concerts, however, and the group had been on two national tours and was going to leave for Europe next month. I figured the in-person popularity was due to the fact that each member of the Whispers was drop dead gorgeous. And Jim had a lusty, raspy voice before anyone ever heard of Rod Stewart.

Jim knew Dan and was surprised I had been living with him. He told me I could do better and proved it to me. We spent the next few weeks together and parted company by laughing at what Jim had told me years before, during my jailbait youth. "Don't ever be afraid of me," he'd said. "It'll never happen with me, baby." I wished Jim well, and he told me to stay safe and take care of Angie. I promised I would.

Warpath returned, and it wasn't long before Dan found me. Too many people knew me, and most thought Dan and I were actually married. The knife that Dan wore on his belt started to come out. He sliced his own arms; he sliced mine. Nasty little cuts. Larry took me to the free clinic, where a post-grad student from UCLA was starting a sensitivity group. No one else in the group was being physically abused, but I met wonderful sad shreds of people. We quickly became a great support system.

One night Sue took the kids out for dinner. I'd taken on longer work hours and arrived home after seven. Everything was dark and quiet. I opened the front door, walked in, laid down my stuff, and headed for the bedroom. Dan was standing there, framed against the moonlit windows, with that damned knife out. He grabbed me by the throat and cut my clothes off. Then he slammed me face down on the bed, held the knife tip to the back of my neck, and had brutal sex with me. When he finally let me up, I just stared at him. I could feel blood on my thighs and I was bruised and hoarse. He looked me up and down saying, "I thought you'd like it." I continued to stare. He spit in my face. That night there was a cop at the free clinic. I gave him Dan's name and address.

Our next door neighbors were bikers. His name was Brutus (after the Popeye comic character) and his wife was Candy, a nude dancer. They had a daughter, Brandy. That name continually struck me funny, and I wondered what on earth possessed these people to name their child after liquor. But they turned out to be the best neighbors I ever had. The whole family decided to put themselves on call 24/7 in case Dan dared to show up again.

Brutus figured out that Dan had gotten into the apartment by slipping the louvers out of my bedroom window, climbing through, and replacing the glass. Brutus put a lock on the inside for me and checked the other entrances. For awhile I thought I was safe.

Chapter Nineteen

"There's Plenty of Room at the Hotel California"
The Eagles

For somebody living on chemical cocktails, Dan had an incredible ability to track me down. Sue and I, and the kids, moved seven times in less than six months. Once we felt settled, we gave our address to exactly six people. So when Rita phoned and said she needed a break from her new husband and infant son, Sue and I agreed to meet her at Hamburger Hamlet. As we sat bouncing garbanzo beans off the sidewalk below, Sue spotted a guy coming up the street.

He was familiar, but I'd never seen him up close. He was short, built, had an unusual but somehow attractive face, and long curly blond hair. All three of us decided he was gorgeous. Someone at a neighboring table said, "Oh look, that's Tommy," and I realized who he was. He was one of several male groupies, a bi-sexual who slept with just about anybody who was somebody. "God," Sue said, "he sure makes Rodney Bingenheimer look like crap," and we all agreed. Word had it Tommy was living with a popular topless dancer, Ginny Galore. Ginny was incredibly ugly but would go completely nude when asked and has been "honored" with inventing the earliest version of the lap dance.

Tommy strutted into Hamburger Hamlet and sat down. I looked at him and thought he was the sexiest thing since Mick Jagger, one of the guys Tommy had apparently slept with. Tommy caught me looking at him, and started staring back. I stopped eating. He ordered a sandwich of some kind, but continued staring at me. When Rita got up to use the restroom, Tommy grabbed her arm. She returned to our table with the news that Tommy wanted to know if I was "free." I asked a waiter to tell Tommy I'd cost him a hundred bucks. The waiter returned with two fifty-dollar bills. Tommy waved me to his table and I walked over, sat down, and offered him his two fifties. He told me to keep them. He just wanted me to read his cards.

The manager tried to scare up Tarot cards, but nobody had any to offer, so we settled for a deck of playing cards. I laid out a traditional Celtic Cross and told Tommy he was heading for a major upheaval. Then he took the deck and laid out cards for me. Both the queen of hearts and the queen of diamonds turned up. "Which one are you?" he asked. I told him I didn't know, and he told me he was going to find out. I thought *How cliché*, but sat waiting to see what he'd do next.

What was I doing? Tommy wasn't a musician. He'd probably never even picked up a guitar. He told me he didn't live with Ginny anymore; he was staying with a stripper named Carol. The sane part of me thought, *Wow, classy guy*. He didn't own or drive a car. He was a philosophy major at UCLA. He loved guys. He loved women. He loved drugs. And he loved rock and roll. He wasn't a music maker. He wasn't anything I wanted in a man. But I was fascinated.

Sue joined us, and then Rita finished her Coke and pulled up a chair. Sue was falling all over herself. I'd never seen her like this. We left the Strip that day in stony silence. None of us had any reason to trust Tommy, and Sue had given him our address.

Cathi called and asked if I wanted to see *Hair* again at the Aquarius Theater (formerly the Hullaballoo). We went to a Sunday matinee. Ted Neeley (formerly of the Teddy Neeley Five) was playing the lead. The cast was marvelous, and the show was great as always. Afterward we went out to eat, and Cathi told me she was getting serious about Rob. What a small world. Rob had grown up two streets away from me. We'd gone all through grade school and high school together, yet Cathi hooked up with him backstage at a concert. I wished Cathi well. She'd lost her mother and her father was ill, but Rob was in her life. Cathi and I both knew life could be strangely fascinating if you weren't afraid to get out there and live it.

The next day Cathi called again, screaming. She told me to turn on the radio. National Guardsmen, banking the Kent State campus during a protest, had opened fire, murdering four innocent students. The Guardsmen claimed to have "mistakenly" heard the command to shoot. Cathi was sucking in little breaths of air. I set down the receiver, tipped my head back, and screamed for a solid minute. Cathi and I swore to get together and talk about life. How far did we want to go with the flower child lifestyle? Did we need college? Did either of us really want marriage?

True to her word, Cathi phoned a week later, but she was in tears. Her father had been drinking, stumbled, and hit his head. He wasn't expected to live.

I went to Cathi's father's funeral with Angie in tow. Rita arrived late, dressed to the nines, driving a new sportscar. Her son was nowhere to be seen. She gave Cathi an air kiss and offered me her fingertips, theoretically for a handshake. I wanted to bite them. Who the hell did she think she was? Cathi had stood up well at her mother's funeral, but today was leaning heavily on Rob. I stayed a few pews back with Cheryl and Rita. Angie sat with her hands folded in her lap, her head against my shoulder. She liked Cathi and understood that the man in the box was Mr. Willard. When Cathi's dad was lowered into the ground on the green tapes, Angie looked in the hole and said, "Goodbye, Mr. Willard. Say hi to your wife," and we walked away.

A couple of weeks later, Tommy showed up at the apartment. He'd brought a friend. Against my will, Sue let the guys in. Tommy introduced Tony, who was originally from San Francisco and had stood in with several of the Frisco bands. Tony drove an expensive new car and carried a deck of Tarot cards. I thought he was trying too hard to be cool; something just wasn't right about him.

After the kids were in bed, Sue broke open a bottle of wine. Alcohol was legal, and we knew little about Tommy and less about Tony. I told Sue if she tried to light a joint, I'd take Angie and leave. She grudgingly agreed to stick to wine. I still didn't drink, but everyone else polished off almost three bottles, and none of them were feeling any pain. I was bored and still feeling annoyed.

Tommy had been staring at me all night, but around midnight, he and Sue went into the bedroom. And they got noisy. When Tony asked if I wanted to screw I said I was tired. I turned on the TV and consumed most of a box of Van de Kamp's chocolate chip cookies before falling asleep.

When the guys left in the morning, Sue told me it had been "the best sex ever." God, she could be irritating.

Tommy brought Tony over two more times that week. He tied up the bedroom going at it with Sue all night, which forced me to try to ignore Tony and sleep on the sofa. I had to be up at five each morning for work, and this was getting very old very fast. The next Friday night, the two guys showed up again. I phoned Larry and Greg and asked if they could be bribed to track down a couple of reds. I was breaking my own No Drugs rule again, but figured that knocking myself out was better than punching out Sue.

An hour later, Larry brought me two reds gift wrapped in a small jewel box. I took them immediately, kissed Larry, and told him I owed him one. In the morning I woke up nude, with Tony next to me. It was time to reassess life.

Cathi phoned. I groaned, "Oh God, who died now?" and she said, "Rob." I told her not to joke like that, and she said she wasn't kidding. Rob had been on his way to work, in a left-hand turn lane, when the light turned red. The woman in front of him decided to back up and plowed right into Rob. He lasted a few days in the hospital, and it looked like he was coming out of the coma, when a nurse found him dead. Somehow he'd banged his head on the bed frame and it killed him. Those of us who knew and loved Rob were convinced that Rob regained consciousness, realized he'd never be the same, and did what he could to end his life.

The funeral was huge. Half of South High was there; alumni, parents, and teachers came. And half of the Strip was there; fellow workers and friends all showed up. A small group of us gathered after the funeral and decided Rob just didn't need to be on the planet anymore. He was that special.

Cathi had lost both of her parents and the love of her life within two years. None of us knew how to help her. But resilient as always, Cathi got herself together, took time off from work, and left to backpack through Europe for a couple of months.

A girl named Sherry was housesitting for Cathi, and one day she gave me a call. Sherry was another Canyon girl, but for some reason we'd never met. She had been invited on a road trip to San Francisco for a week but had a daughter Angie's age and didn't think it was smart to take her along. Cathi had left my name and number as a resource. Sherry asked me for the name of a good babysitter. I told her that Sue babysat for a living and to bring Cory over. When I wasn't at work, I'd tend to Cory myself; she could bunk with Angie.

Sherry walked through the door, long blond hair and pouty lips, tight jeans, and a suede shoulder bag with fringe brushing the floor. She seemed stunned to meet me. I eventually got my breath and welcomed her in. I was having an intense sexual response to her, something that was unfamiliar to me. Angie and Cory tottered into the other room to play, and Sherry and I sat down to talk. She gave me a copy of her itinerary and contact information in case of emergency. I told her not to worry; Cory would be fine. Before Sherry left, she hugged me. It was a long hug. Then she gave me a peck on the lips, something that turned into a real kiss. We stared at each other for a long time before letting go.

Tommy learned I was sticking close to home, babysitting. He dropped by late Monday afternoon. I'd gotten home from work and taken charge of the kids while Sue went to the supermarket. Tommy and I talked about people we knew, people we'd slept with, and how we perceived the whole Hollywood scene. I made a comment about how much Sue liked him. He laughed and said, "Damn, she's a pain in the ass, that's a lot of fat to wade through." That was the last thing I expected to hear. He'd been sleeping with Sue for two weeks and seemed to be enjoying himself.

I put the kids down for a nap and asked Tommy to leave. He told me I didn't want him to leave. I replied that yes, I did. He said okay, but that he'd be back that night. I muttered something about not being Sue's keeper, and he left.

Sure enough, he showed up about seven, but with a different friend. He introduced David to Sue and told them they needed to talk because they had a lot in common. Sue looked confused. Later, when she tried to coax Tommy into the bedroom, he refused to go. She asked him what was wrong and he said, "It's been fun, let's leave it at that." Sue responded by taking David into the bedroom and closing the door. The kids were asleep and I was going to spend another night on the sofa. I wasn't happy.

Tommy started chatting and I began to understand what made him so popular. He could get to you. By ten o'clock, we were having sex on the living room floor. Suddenly he hesitated and laughed. When I asked him what was so funny, he said, "I knew if I held out long enough and played my cards right, I'd nail you. Damn. I'm finally screwing Sally." Normally I would have been offended, but for some reason it struck me funny.

Within the month, I learned that Tony had been arrested for embezzlement, and Tommy and I moved into our own place. Tommy lived with me for several years. He did his thing and I did mine, but almost every night, once Angela was asleep, we had incredible sex.

Chapter Twenty

"This Is the End, Beautiful Friend, the End"
The Doors

Six months after getting back from Europe, Cathi announced her engagement to an older man, a corporate executive. The rest of us were stunned. She was one of us! She was going to marry a musician! She was into sex, drugs, and rock and roll. Sherry and I were asked to be her bridesmaids in a traditional Catholic wedding. We both agreed. We also agreed that Cathi was trying to replace her parents with this nerd.

Cathi and Sherry came over to my place the day before the wedding. Sherry was going to spend the night at Cathi's, then the three of us were going to get our hair done for the wedding. When Cathi left for the bathroom, Sherry grabbed my hands and asked if Tommy was coming home that night. I told her he was on tour for the week with a popular group. She asked if she could spend the night with me and, oh God, I wanted her to.

Cathi wouldn't hear of it. If we wouldn't both spend the night at her house, at least Sherry was obligated to. After all, it was Cathi's day. She was getting married tomorrow.

Sherry and I changed into our bridesmaid garb in a small upstairs room at the church. The two of us were alone, guiltily making bets about how long Cathi's marriage would last. Sherry felt her period coming on, and said she didn't want to be rude but needed to insert a Tampax. I turned to tell her it was fine, and we stared at each other, naked. Sherry leaned in to kiss me just before we heard the rustle of taffeta and lace, and Cathi's voice shouting for us to hurry up.

The wedding was beautiful and Cathi seemed happy. She and Jim were going to drive to Canada for their honeymoon. We all wished them well. Sherry left for home, promising to call me. We talked on the phone nearly every day, had lunch together about once a week, and planned to spend the night together two different times. Each time, Sherry's live-in boyfriend hid her car keys. We finally chose a night for me to drive to her place. When I drove up, the boyfriend was standing on the front porch, arms crossed, shaking his head. I talked to Sherry one last time. She was scared. The boyfriend had sent her to the hospital twice, after accusing her of infidelity with a couple of men she didn't even know. Several weeks later, Cathi phoned me with the news that someone had put a hit out on Cory. About a month after that, we heard that Sherry and Cory had gone missing. Nobody ever heard from either of them again.

I was tired of Tommy and started letting Angie stay with my sister and her family on weekends. Ann liked Angie, and our kids got along great. The world was making the transition from the sixties to the seventies and a lot of newer, younger rock musicians were on the Strip, along with a whole herd of folk-rock singers. I liked the music, but I didn't like what was happening to some of the older guys who felt like a new generation and genre was taking over, pushing them out. Drug-related deaths were becoming common among those original rock musicians.

On one hot afternoon, Cathi phoned to tell me she'd run into Joe. He had moved out of Laurel Canyon and into the apartment building next to the Aquarius Theater. Cathi was full of strange, very personal gossip about Joe, none of which sounded like the man I knew. Cathi gave me the new phone number, and Joe confirmed some of what I'd heard and denied the rest. Something was wrong; I'd never before known Joe to be contradictory like he was now. I started to say that if, for whatever reason, he needed me for moral or financial support, I'd be there. But Joe was still talking, throwing me a last bone by encouraging me to join the new group of folk-rock singer-songwriters taking over the Canyon. Joe didn't ask how I was doing, and nothing was said about our former physical attraction or our longtime friendship. That final conversation broke my heart. I loved that man.

The hippies, more precisely the concept of "hippie" itself, was buried in several simultaneous ceremonies across the United States and part of Europe. It was the early seventies, and those of us who had been the original hippies learned it was time to walk our talk and take care of business. We became lawyers, lobbyists, researchers, and writers, because we knew the only way to change society was from the inside. Those ceremonies ended an era that had begun with the assassination of JFK and was ending with the aftermath of Watergate and other signs of destruction. No other decade would ever be able to duplicate the sixties.

A group from the neighborhood got together and bought tickets to see the Moody Blues in Long Beach. It was the first good concert I'd seen in a long time. And this time, we all stayed in our seats. Backstage, there were a lot of people; it was almost a mob scene. I recognized a new folk-rock singer and a couple of older groupies. I managed to meet the guys one by one, and wished each of them well; I was a long-time fan. When I was introduced to Mike, he pulled me in and kissed me. It reminded me of the gentle rock star/groupie activity I'd known years before. A tear ran down my cheek, and Mike asked what was wrong. I told him I was just remembering the way life used to be, that things were changing in the world and I wasn't sure if those changes were good. He said he knew precisely what I meant, and then he hugged me tight for a long minute. I respected the Moody Blues. They were real musicians, and their music moved me. I wouldn't be in the company of another great group for a couple of years.

One afternoon, Sue and I visited Bonnie, a plump and pretty girl Sue had known in high school. She'd moved into a neat little place in the Canyon. On the way home we stopped at the Canyon Store and literally ran into Charley. I stepped back from a refrigerator onto his foot. Oh, I was glad to see him! He was back from Haight-Ashbury (which he hadn't liked), was going to UCLA "a little late," and was working part time at Pandora's Box. Charley introduced me to Suzanne, who looked a lot like me. She gave me a warm smile, took my hands, and said she'd heard a lot about me. She seemed like a sweetheart, and I was happy for Charley and sad for myself at the same time. Charley told me about a hotel party at the Ambassador. He would put Sue's name and my name on the list.

We arrived just before ten. Things looked pretty dead for a hotel party. The door was closed and we could barely hear music playing inside. A big guy answered our knock and asked for our names. He checked us off the list and let us inside.

The atmosphere seemed surprisingly mellow. There were only about two dozen people drifting around, and it looked like everyone was just smoking weed. An hour later Charley and Suzanne arrived, and a group of us gathered to talk. By two in the morning there must have been a hundred people inside and we were getting complaints from other hotel guests. It had finally turned into a typical hotel party. One guy, on some kind of hallucinogenic, had a seizure. A couple of people from a popular group brought electric guitars and an amp. Two years prior I loved big, loud parties like this, but that night I felt nervous and claustrophobic.

I wanted to leave, but couldn't find Sue. A guy I'd seen at the Troubadour several times was sitting in a corner with his own pipe and bag of weed. I joined him. We talked for a couple of hours. Yes, it looked like we were finally getting out of Vietnam. Yes, women needed equal rights. Yes, abortion should be legalized and marijuana needed to be de-criminalized. Yes, civil rights was a major issue. Although our generation was idealistic and our hopes remained high, life in general seemed to be taking a downward spiral. If we could have predicted disco, preppies, and yuppies, we would probably both have given up then and there. As we were moaning about the fate of the world, a girl smashed her head and arms through a closed window. Hotel security wrapped her in a blanket and took her away as a favor to one major rock star who'd shown up. There was blood everywhere and shortly we heard the siren of an ambulance.

Sue showed up toward morning. She looked sick and had bruises on her face and arms. I told her we had to retrieve the kids from her mother, piled her in the car, and asked her what happened. She didn't remember. She had shared a drink with somebody, and woke up in pain. Later, when Sue got in the shower, she called me into the bathroom. There was a half-dollar sized pentagram carved into the side of her left breast. It was frighteningly deep and was still oozing. The clothes she'd been wearing were stained with blood. We went to the free clinic and explained what happened. The doctor took care of the wound and gave Sue a tetanus shot and antibiotics. That was my last hotel party.

On a dreary afternoon a week later, my sister phoned. Mom was in intensive care and the doctors wanted the family to come and say goodbye. Mom's liver and kidneys had shut down; her primary doctor said she couldn't possibly survive. Sue and I drove to Ann's, where Sue took charge of all the kids. Ann and I went to the hospital. Mom had just been brought back from some sort of test. As I stood by her bed, she moaned, "That was the worst test I've ever had." I asked if she wanted anything, and she dismissed me with a characteristically abrupt, "I just want to go to sleep." Mom somehow survived, and went on to spread her own unique brand of charm for another another forty years.

Chapter Twenty-One

"See Me Fly Away Without You"
Neil Young

Tommy's lifestyle was taking its toll on him, and he started to age right before my eyes. People didn't want to take him on tour anymore. UCLA dumped him. His solution was to stay stoned.

I wanted him to leave. College was in my future, hopefully a degree in either music or theater. I wanted to be in the business. If I couldn't directly make the music I loved, I at least wanted to be part of the scene. And here I was with a guy whose only contribution to the household had been that first hundred dollars, years ago. He never paid a bill. He never washed a dish. He refused to babysit. And the burden of supporting him and his habits had left me in a house with no heat and no phone. I had to turn things around. With Donna's help, that was about to happen. She let me know that Capitol Records needed someone with steno/typing skills, a knowledge of music, and the ability to deal one-on-one with musicians. Not only was I the first person who came to her mind, I was the only one.

Before committing to anything, I went to the free clinic to find out if I was anemic again. I'd been involved with the free clinic for several years and had met some great doctors. It was a wonderful, safe place to go for those of us living on limited means.

A doctor led me into a room and remarked that I looked pale. I told her I was under a lot of stress and had a history of anemia. She asked if I'd ever had mono, and I groaned that I had. She spent a lot of time with me. It had been awhile since I'd really been checked over. When she gave me my pelvic exam she asked, "How far along are you?" to which I responded, "What?!" I told her I wasn't pregnant; I'd been using a diaphragm for years. She told me she didn't care if I was the Virgin Mary. I was pregnant.

Roe versus Wade had passed, and abortion was legal. I made an appointment with a doctor, and he set up a time for Friday. I was at the end of my first trimester, the cut-off point. Larry and Greg, my gay friends, agreed to take me in and stay with me. Sue would babysit. We got to the hospital ten minutes early and I signed in. Fifteen minutes later, a nurse told me my doctor was attending to a family emergency and that I'd have to go home and reschedule.

It was the last day of my first trimester. I couldn't reschedule. Wasn't there somebody else? Didn't she understand that I'd given up one child and was caring for another? Abortion was legal, damn it! Larry and Greg piled me into the car. We drove all over town, checking with doctors for referrals. I'd chosen one of just a small handful of abortionists in the Los Angeles area, and all were booked solid. Greg hadn't been feeling well and was scheduled for a minor surgery, so Larry drove. Greg held me tight all the way home.

I stopped eating. I dragged Angie to Sue's house in the mornings and then dragged myself to work. Donna said Capitol was willing to wait through my "illness" because they couldn't find anyone better qualified. I didn't speak to Tommy, whose permanent response to the word *pregnancy* was "I don't care how you do it, just get rid of it." I started taking fewer jobs until I just couldn't work at all; I was too tired to stay upright all day. Sue borrowed the Nash, and kept it. I concentrated on taking care of Angie; she was my sole focus. One night I found that the cupboards were literally bare. There was enough milk to give Angie one glass. I had a quarter and some pennies in my purse. I'd used my emergency boot fund.

I walked to the corner store and laid down change for a box of Angie's favorite meatless noodles Romanoff. Back home, I boiled water and poured in the contents of the box. It was full of bugs. Angie told me not to worry and ran to a neighbor up the street. She came back with a can of split pea soup. She told me Eva and Isaac's mommy knew I was sick and that if I needed to borrow anything else, to let them know now because they were going on vacation.

Later that night, I got a sharp pain and started bleeding. It lasted the night and stopped. The next morning Rita dropped by on her way to visit her father. She told me her husband had been killed in a mysterious accident and left her with a pile of insurance money. She'd already staked out husband number two. I told her I'd had some pain and bleeding, but she didn't seem to think I should worry. I asked her if I could borrow a few dollars. She handed me three bucks, claiming it was all she had on her; I didn't believe her for a minute. I rushed to borrow the neighbor's phone before they left on vacation, and called the free clinic. The doctor I typically saw told me to go to a hospital. I piled Angie and my purse onto a bus and went to the ER. I explained that I'd been through two childbirths and that I was in labor. They told me I had a bladder infection and sent me home with a huge bill to pay.

The following morning my water broke. Tommy was asleep. I woke him up and told him I needed to get to a hospital. When he saw what was happening he told me he couldn't deal with it, showered, and left. I dressed Angie and walked to the nearest payphone. It was out of order. We went four city blocks before I found a working phone.

Sue didn't want to bring the car back. She was having a party, which apparently had been going on all week. I said fine, she could keep it, but I was going to phone the cops and report it stolen. About an hour later, she showed up, semi-sober, and dropped off the Nash. She jumped into the back of a pickup truck without so much as a goodbye.

There was a hospital a couple of miles away. I propped myself up in the driver's seat, but told Angie she needed to help me by keeping her hands next to mine on the steering wheel and watching out for any reason to stop. At the emergency entrance, a nurse brought a wheelchair and a security guard parked the Nash. A candy striper asked what she could do to help. I asked her to phone my sister, who promised to pick up Angie. While waiting, the candy striper assured Angie I was going to be fine and kept her entertained with an amazing talent for origami. I told the nurses I didn't want any drugs, and they respected me. They said it would be awhile before a doctor could get tend to me. The woman in the bed next to me was trying to eat lunch and I kept apologizing for cursing and gasping my way through labor pains while she ate. She just laughed. She had seven kids and had been through as many miscarriages. That woman was great, cracking rude jokes and keeping my spirits up. I told her about Tommy, and she told me at least I wouldn't be giving live birth to a demon child. She actually made me laugh.

Even with today's technology, the baby couldn't have been saved. I was almost six months along, but it was a stillborn miscarriage. It happened right there in the hospital bed and as soon as I rang for the nurse, a whole tribe of them rushed in to take a look. I really didn't care. It was over.

I was malnourished, dehydrated, and needed a D&C. They decided to keep me in the hospital two nights. Nobody phoned. Nobody stopped by. My sister called my aunt and told her what was going on. When I was released from the hospital, my aunt and my father picked me up, Angie in tow. She was happy to see me. I wasn't supposed to drive for a few days, so Daddy drove the Nash back to my place, and my aunt stopped so I could fill my shiny new prescription for birth control pills.

When I got home, Tommy was there. He told me it had been nice having me out of the house. I reminded him I was the sole breadwinner and that it was my place. He was welcome to leave anytime. Then I noticed some serious-looking burns on his face. A candle I'd made and had burned the week prior to the miscarriage had coincidentally exploded in his face, singeing off his eyebrows and eyelashes and burning his forehead. I said, "Don't ever mess with me again." It was the only time I ever saw fear cross Tommy's face.

He wouldn't go away. Now that nobody else wanted him, he tried to convince me that we were soulmates, that I needed him, that nobody else would ever want me, even that I was legally insane. He was desperate. I spent the next few months of this ridiculous relationship ignoring him as best I could.

In an attempt to shift the energy, I moved into a different apartment, but Tommy just tagged along.

Although I didn't trust Sue like I did once, I started going to concerts with her. Anything was better than being at home with Tommy. Sue's mother was always willing to babysit and the kids loved her. We were back in the Hollywood scene, and it felt good. Katy was in San Francisco with a big-time drug dealer; Rita had convinced her latest to divorce his pregnant wife; Cathi had divorced Jim and was growing marijuana in a gorgeous garden behind her house. Greg had died from surgical complications, Gail had given birth to child number two in Canada, Joe still lived in the same apartment with his new wife, and Garry the Wind had died in Vietnam. Larry was sent to jail for refusing the draft. The draft board did not believe that my effeminate little daisy of a friend was actually gay. Folk-rock concerts were full of kids who wanted to stand up and dance. Things were continuing to change in a way that didn't appeal to me at all.

Since two months before the miscarriage, we'd been living on peanut butter and brown rice. I was finally feeling more like myself again, and Capitol Records had, miraculously, held the job for me. Sue's sister was going to babysit Angie during the day but called that first morning to tell me she'd gotten stuck and would be an hour late. I needed Tommy to babysit, and tracked him down at a crack house on Doheny. When I told him I had to be at Capitol on time, he laughed at me. I reached for him, and he grabbed my arm and twisted it behind my back. I heard two snaps. I got back in the car and tried to grasp the wheel, but my right hand just hung there. Using my left arm and my legs, I steered that faithful old Nash to the nearest clinic. Angie patted my arm the whole way, telling me it was all right.

Sure enough, Tommy had broken my wrist and my thumb. I was going to be stuck in a cast for six weeks. Donna, at the temp agency, told me I needed an exorcist and phoned Capitol. They'd wait. Apparently they were hanging onto my resume' with a death grip. I didn't know what to do in the meantime. Tommy had never worked a day in his life and was now taking money from me for drugs.

I went to Angie's school. We were below poverty level, so she was given lunch tickets. At least she'd have one meal a day. I sold my good work clothes to a couple of girls in the building. We were still on peanut butter and brown rice.

Eventually the cast came off. I settled in at Capitol; the lunch tickets ended; and I bought new work clothes. Ten Years After was going to be in L.A., and I bought tickets for Sue and me. Cathi, already divorced, introduced me to her latest love, and the three of us started hanging out at the Whiskey again. I found a great jazz dance class at the Cabaret Theatre. Things were beginning to look up. But Tommy still came around, almost every night.

One Saturday I had a special job. It was personal office work for a professor I knew, and the woman allowed me to bring Angie. I felt sick all day, and by the time we got home, I had dry heaves. When I looked in the mirror my cheeks were blotchy and my eyes hollow. Tommy came in, looked at me, and started laughing. My hands were shaking so badly that I smashed my fingers trying to break up some ice cubes. That also struck him funny. I tried to lie down, but when I did, I couldn't breathe.

I phoned Sue and told her I needed to get to a hospital. My vision was blurred, and I couldn't drive. After an argument that ended with me pleading, Sue hung up on me. I phoned my sister, but no one was home. I was going to have to drive, so I called my aunt, who said she'd get to the hospital as soon as possible and take Angie home with her; my mother be damned.

I drove looking through the gray tunnel that was now my visual field. The ER doctor checked me over and told me he couldn't find anything wrong. I burst into tears. He told me he knew I was sick, I just didn't have anything like the flu. In his private office he asked about my life. I told him what had happened in the recent past and what was going on now. He said, "Tell you what I'm going to do. You find a babysitter for your little girl. I'm going to admit you as having a severe case of the flu, because all policies cover severe flu. With your new insurance, we ought to be able to keep you a couple of weeks." I reminded him that he'd said I didn't have the flu, that I was fine. He told me I wasn't. I had "nervous exhaustion," also known as a nervous breakdown.

Aside from my aunt, the only people who knew where I was were Sue and Tommy. Sue stopped by to borrow my car again. I told her to screw herself. Tommy's sister stopped by looking for Tommy. I told her to check hell; I was sure he'd show up there sooner or later. A nurse got me access to a phone. I called Donna and Capitol and was told by both to get well; my job was safe. I phoned my aunt to check on Angie. Es promised to visit that night. When she showed up, she told me Cathi had been trying to reach me. She referred to a piece of paper. Charley had phoned around until he reached Cathi. Cat Stevens had a one-night local gig. Charley said Cat and his crew heard a tape Joe and I had made years earlier; they liked my lyrics and my sound. Cathi had backstage passes for the two of us. I was supposed to bring my guitar.

When I was released from the hospital two restful weeks later, Es followed me back to the apartment to make sure I arrived safely. I asked the manager to check and see if Tommy was there. The coast was clear. I phoned friends and told them I'd be in touch within the week. When I reached Larry, he said he couldn't stand the house since Greg had died and asked if Angie and I would room with him. I packed some of Angie's clothes, jeans and work clothes for myself, and Angie's books and toys. They went in the trunk. My guitar went in the backseat with my overnight bag and a box of bottled drinks and munchies.

I phoned to have the utilities turned off, ripped the phone out of the wall, and left a note for Tommy, letting him know the rent was paid until the first.

Then Angie and I climbed into the Nash. I had solid work at Capitol and was meeting interesting people every day. Larry sounded genuinely relieved to have Angie and me moving in. Angie excitedly asked where we were going. I told her we were moving in with Larry, and that I was going on a big hunt for real music. She asked which music. I told her I was going to talk to Cat Stevens. Angie said, "Moonshadow?" I nodded. She clapped her hands. I had my driver's license and money in my boot. All we had to do was drive away.

Afterword

"The Long and Winding Road"
The Beatles

I walk down the Strip today, in my jeans, boots, and somewhat upscaled version of a T-shirt, hair still long and makeup intact, and see kids scribbling graffiti, hear them threatening parents and shopkeepers, and cringe at the negativity hanging thick in the air. Religious and political zealots don't just hand out incense and fliers, they scream from streetcorners and, if not given attention, slam their hands on car hoods like Ratso Rizzo in *Midnight Cowboy*. The Canyon has become more of an upscale neighborhood for celebrities than a haven for the music crowd. The Canyon Store, formerly just the local mini-mart, sells T-shirts promoting its landmark status.

Much modern sound isn't music. It's violent, sexist, unnecessarily obscene racist noise, produced by greed-driven celebrities rather than musicians. It is completely and utterly devoid of soul. New rock, however, is reminiscent of original rock, and is beautifully produced by serious musicians with plenty to say about the state of the world, and about love.

The most obvious change in the culture is a complete lack of respect. There is no respect for the world, one's country, people in positions of authority, family, peers, or even self. Children are raised either to take care of themselves completely, to make them "tough," or they are so horribly smothered they don't know how to deal with the world without being told. Socio-political "correctness" has taken away our freedom of speech and freedom of the press. Children following the abominable precedent set by child actor Gary Coleman are suing parents and teachers for attempting to take care of business. The government passed "corrupt" decades ago and is heading toward a downfall. In my subjective and humble opinion, we need a revolution.

We have become so insular we don't see beyond our computer screens, and wouldn't care even if we bothered to take a look. The spiritual awakening of the sixties has been corrupted by greed-driven modern gurus who draw in followers with re-hashes of ancient philosophies, and then sell those people programs, seminars, retreats, DVD collections, workshops, book series, inspirational coffee mugs, affirmation cards, and stones with words stamped on them. Those being misguided in their own searches for spirituality are offset by right-wing fundamentalists who have interpreted the Bible to suit their causes, whatever those may be. I've had people at my door asking me to help overturn Roe versus Wade, to help provide even greater tax breaks for churches (no matter how small the congregation), and to help stop animal control from allowing public adoption of pure-bred dogs because God wants to keep those blood lines pure. God seems to be talking to everyone and giving each person completely contradictory advice.

Readers can dispute everything I just said, but one thing I guarantee everyone will agree with after sixty years on this planet is that people don't change.

Jeanne is a multi-millionaire attorney living in an exclusive suburb of Los Angeles. She married the first man who asked her on a date, at the age of twenty-nine. She has nothing to do with friends from her past.

Katy found her match and has been happily married for over thirty years. She lives up north and runs a travel agency. Katy remains a good friend, but doesn't like to talk about the old days.

Linda nabbed a cute younger husband and lives up north near Katy. She has an amazing memory for silly things we did as kids.

Willy spent almost a decade in England and swears he'd retire there if he could do so legally. He's an antiques dealer and lives nearby with his three dogs. Aside from e-mails and occasional visits, Willy usually keeps to himself.

I last heard from Cathi in the 1980s. She was happily married to husband number two, and working as a CPA.

Rita hooked that married guy she was after, pulled some underhanded stunts to set him up in a failproof business, and is now considered one of Southern California's socialites. We may not approve of each other's social and political ideas, but there's still a spark of the old Rita in there somewhere. You can take the girl out of the Canyon, but you can't take the Canyon out of the girl.

Yvette apparently worked at Michael Jackson's Neverland for many years, and is now living in a fabulous beach house in Malibu. We all knew she'd make it big.

Dinah is married to a blind man. They live below poverty level in the mid-west, and hope to move back to California.

Sue was married to a great guy for decades, but is now widowed. Fortunately, she lives surrounded by family.

Dan legally divorced me "just to be sure" and was obligated to pay child support. I never saw a cent. He has a long record of assault and battery, and his emphysema keeps him on oxygen 24/7. He supplements his disability checks by marrying (and later divorcing) Eastern European women wanting into the United States.

Tommy, unable to get a job or a date, ended up joining the army. After a couple of years he became plagued with health problems. Despite internal bleeding, a bout with cancer, diabetes, and other issues, he has continued to track me down and harass me. Although he has proposed to several women, myself included, no one has ever agreed to marry him. He's back in California, taking disability from the United States government. He lives with his mother.

I last heard from Charley and his wife during the late 1970s. He was finishing his master's degree in sociology at UCLA, and a pregnant Suzanne was writing a children's book.

My sister, Ann, is retired and living happily with her second husband in the wilds of Oregon. My brother, Paul, lives in L.A. and has a hot-shot job with Dreamworks. My daughter, Angie, survived her own years on the Strip and has gone back to school at mid-life for her doctorate in psychology.

My grandmother died peacefully at eighty-eight, in the early 1970s. My aunt Es made it to age eighty-six, when she passed away in her sleep. My father lived to be ninety-three, and was gone after just three days of pneumonia. My mother was hospitalized and mistakenly hooked up to life support for a week before anyone found out. The whole family went to see her the day Daddy ordered the tubes and needles removed. I remember staring into her huge dark eyes that held me, and only me, in their stare. Unable to speak, she was still trying to communicate. The following day, Angie phoned to say Mom was dead. I've never shed one tear.

The Nash was with me until the mid-1970s, when the exhaust system suddenly and completely gave out. I sold her to a garage mechanic for a hundred bucks. He made the necessary repairs and re-sold the car. The Nash was still seen cruising the streets of the beach cities in the late 1980s.

I look at my friends and realize that with the exception of Rita, we're all still socially open-minded, politically liberal, and spiritually free-thinking. We stuck to our belief in civil rights, the environment, and Zero Population Growth (now called Population Connection). Jeanne, Rita, Sue, Gail, and I are the only members of the old group who chose to have children. We e-mail petitions and other relevant socio-political material. We're aware, and try to provoke some sense of consciousness in others. And when we get together, it's a sea of denim.

I'm back at the beach, not too far from where I grew up. That meeting backstage at the Cat Stevens concert oddly enough got me involved in L.A. rock music theater, where I wrote, performed, and (after college) taught for decades. Having survived a twenty-year marriage and heart disease, I now edit other people's musicals. I'll turn sixty just about the time this book is published, and if I die that day, at least I'll know I lived in a most incredible time. There will never again be a decade so remarkably transitional, terrifying, and beautiful as the sixties.

3394042

Made in the USA